SPOOKY
Colorado

*Tales of Hauntings, Strange Happenings,
and Other Local Lore*

RETOLD BY S. E. SCHLOSSER

ILLUSTRATED BY PAUL G. HOFFMAN

gpp

Guilford, Connecticut

To buy books in quantity for corporate use
or incentives, call **(800) 962-0973**
or e-mail **premiums@GlobePequot.com.**

Project editor: Meredith Dias
Layout: Joanna Beyer
Text design: Lisa Reneson, Two Sisters Design
Map: Daniel Lloyd © Morris Book Publishing, LLC

Library of Congress Cataloging-in-Publication Data
Schlosser, S. E.
  Spooky Colorado : tales of hauntings, strange happenings, and other local lore / retold by S.E. Schlosser ; illustrated by Paul G. Hoffman.
    p. cm.
  ISBN 978-0-7627-6410-5
  1. Ghosts—Colorado. 2. Haunted places—Colorado. I. Hoffman, Paul G. II. Title.
  BF1472.U6S293 2011
  398.209788'05—dc23

                                              2011019087

Printed in the United States of America

10 9 8 7 6 5 4 3 2

SPOOKY

Colorado

Also in the Spooky Series by
S. E. Schlosser and Paul G. Hoffman:

Spooky California
Spooky Campfire Tales
Spooky Canada
Spooky Florida
Spooky Maryland
Spooky Massachusetts
Spooky Michigan
Spooky Montana
Spooky New England
Spooky New Jersey
Spooky New York
Spooky North Carolina
Spooky Oregon
Spooky Pennsylvania
Spooky South
Spooky South Carolina
Spooky Southwest
Spooky Texas
Spooky Virginia
Spooky Washington
Spooky Wisconsin

For my family: David, Dena, Tim, Arlene, Hannah, Emma, Nathan, Ben, Deb, Gabe, Clare, Jack, Chris, Karen, Davey, and Aunt Mil.

For Erin Turner, Paul Hoffman, and all the wonderful folks at Globe Pequot Press, with my thanks.

Contents

MAP   viii

INTRODUCTION   xi

PART ONE: GHOST STORIES

1.   *A Whitewashed Privy*   2
CENTRAL CITY

2.   *A Friendly Game of Cards*   10
JULESBURG

3.   *Dunraven*   15
ESTES PARK

4.   *Spirit Guide*   22
MANITOU SPRINGS

5.   *Dead Man's Canyon*   29
NEAR COLORADO SPRINGS

6.   *Rented Rooms*   36
DENVER

7.   *Empty Bucket*   42
LEADVILLE

8.   *The Piper*   48
TELLURIDE

9.   *Man in the Derby Hat*   55
GOLDEN

10.   *The White Lady*   61
GRAND JUNCTION

11.   *Maggie*   67
CRIPPLE CREEK

12.   *Vindicator*   72
SAND CREEK MASSACRE NATIONAL HISTORIC SITE

SPOOKY SITES . . .

1. Central City
2. Julesburg
3. Estes Park
4. Manitou Springs
5. Colorado Springs
6. Denver
7. Leadville
8. Telluride
9. Golden
10. Grand Junction
11. Cripple Creek
12. Sand Creek Massacre National Historic Site
13. Palmer Lake

AND WHERE TO FIND THEM

②

㉑

⑨
⑥ ⑰

⑬

④ ⑤

⑫

⑭ Eureka

⑮ Breckenridge

⑯ The Spanish Peaks

⑰ Denver

⑱ Ouray County

⑲ Rico

⑳ Durango

㉑ Fort Collins

㉒ Glenwood Springs

㉓ Silverton

㉔ Gunnison County

㉕ South Park

Contents

PART TWO: POWERS OF DARKNESS AND LIGHT

13. *The Telegram*   80
    PALMER LAKE

14. *Unexpected Witness*   89
    EUREKA

15. *Haunted Spring*   98
    BRECKENRIDGE

16. *La Muñeca*   107
    THE SPANISH PEAKS

17. *Roller Skating*   113
    DENVER

18. *Tom Barren's Cache*   120
    OURAY COUNTY

19. *The Piano Man*   127
    RICO

20. *The Weeper*   133
    DURANGO

21. *The Icehouse*   142
    FORT COLLINS

22. *Doc*   151
    GLENWOOD SPRINGS

23. *Graven Image*   159
    SILVERTON

24. *Snake Totem*   167
    GUNNISON COUNTY

25. *Desperado*   177
    SOUTH PARK

RESOURCES   184
ABOUT THE AUTHOR   190
ABOUT THE ILLUSTRATOR   191

Introduction

The melodic sound of "Ghost Riders in the Sky" floated through the darkening sky as I sipped my coffee and gazed at the red rock formation towering against the sunset. A cumulus cloud above the rock became pink and orange with a saffron underlay as the cowboy song wound on, tugging at my heartstrings.

We'd started the day in Alamosa at the Great Sand Dunes National Park, where we gawked at the largest dunes in the United States, sitting at the base of the mountains with a creek wandering past and mule deer peacefully grazing. Then we drove up into the vastness of the region known as South Park, where the Bloody Espinosa gang robbed freight wagons, stole horses, and murdered many men in their thirst for revenge against the United States, which had won the Mexican–American War and—in the process—had ruined their lives ("Desperado"). In the glorious, hot days of early summer, with the flowers blooming, the snow melting rapidly from the peaks, and the sun shining bright, it was hard to imagine what those months of terror must have been like for the settlers living in South Park and its environs. We had lunch in Salida, stopped for a few hours in Cañon City to ride to the bottom of Royal Gorge, and then made our way to this fabulous dinner at the Flying W Ranch just outside Colorado Springs.

As I listened to western music drifting through the night, my thoughts roamed across Colorado, where I'd spent the last three weeks gathering information for the next installment of

the Spooky series. I'd slept in the haunted Stanley Hotel in Estes Park, the place that inspired the film *The Shining* by Stephen King and where Lord Dunraven still chases the ladies, long after having shed his corporeal remains ("Dunraven"). I'd wandered through Leadville, where a ghost scared a newly hired miner so bad he quit the same day he started ("Empty Bucket"). I bathed in the hot springs of Glenwood Springs, where Doc Holliday breathed his last ("Doc"). And I roamed through Colorado National Monument in Grand Junction, which is adjacent to the canyon where the White Lady walks.

Cripple Creek was next on my *Spooky* agenda. There was a certain Maggie's Restaurant where I planned to have lunch, hoping to smell an old-fashioned floral perfume that heralded the presence of Maggie herself, the ghost for whom the restaurant was named. Then I planned to descend one thousand feet underground in the Molly Kathleen mine to see for myself the mineral that caused the last great Colorado gold rush.

But that was tomorrow. For tonight, I sat on a bench under the wide night sky, dreaming of cowboys and the Wild West and thanking my lucky stars that I hadn't met the ghost in Dead Man's Canyon on my way to Colorado Springs. Unlike the friendly Maggie, that phantom wanders about with an ax through his head and accosts unsuspecting travelers when they enter his turf. No thanks.

I encountered many fabulous stories in my time in Colorado. Ghosts who sent telegrams ("The Telegram"), Tommyknockers who saved one life and took another in the very same mine shaft ("Graven Image"), and of course "A Friendly Game of Cards" played with . . . you guessed it. . . . a ghost! Phantom pipers still play in the mountains ("The Piper"). La Llorona weeps by the river ("The Weeper"). A dead miner guards his cache in a remote canyon ("Tom Barren's Cache"). And a ghost who once haunted "A Whitewashed Privy" continues to plague the plumbing in Central City.

In this moment of carefree joy, eating at the ranch, enjoying the music, seeing the bright faces of the people around me, I knew that Colorado had made an indelible imprint on my heart. From the grandiose Fourteeners to Mesa Verde, from the ghosts in Denver ("Roller Skating") to "The Weeper" in Durango, I fell in love with this state. Hey, Colorado, have you got room for one more?

—Sandy Schlosser

PART ONE
Ghost Stories

1

A Whitewashed Privy

CENTRAL CITY

I was real surprised when the accountant sold me his house in early June 1873 for practically a song. He seemed eager to move and didn't blink an eye at my low bid. It was a nice place, too, just outside Central City, with a fancy whitewashed privy near the creek out back. It was a bit too fancy for my taste, tell you the truth. But love does strange things to a feller. At least, it did them to me.

I was coming up in the world now that I'd used my hard-won gold to buy me a mercantile. When I first proposed to my gal Jessica, she told me she didn't want to marry a miner. No sir. I had to have a respectable job, or she would have nothing to do with me. So I set myself up as a store owner, selling goods to all the scruffy miners in town, and making more money at it than I would have digging for gold. And so Jessica had married me in a frothy white dress she'd whipped up from some of the fabric I sold in my store.

Jessie was plumb taken with our new place and made me paint the house white so it "coordinated" with our fancy privy. Women! I'll never understand them. But to please her, I ordered some white paint, and when it came in, I painted the new house for my bride. She thanked me good and proper for my hard work. Her kisses left me starry-eyed, which earned me some teasing from the men who shopped in the mercantile. But I didn't care. They were just jealous because I'd married me the sweetest gal in the whole country.

About two weeks after we moved into our new house, I was getting ready to retire for the night when I heard Jessie give a terrible holler from the direction of the privy. I grabbed my gun and ran outside in time to see my new wife tumble ungracefully forth, her petticoats awry.

"There's a man in our privy," she shouted when she saw me. She was flushed red right up to her eyebrows, caught midway between embarrassment and rage.

The thought of any man gawking at my new wife's petticoats got me steamed. I raced passed her and banged on the privy, gun at the ready. It was a big privy: a two-holer. And it was empty. Unless the man had slipped down into the muck below—and he hadn't, 'cause I checked—then my wife must have been imagining things.

I walked outside, scratching my head, and said to Jessie: "Honey, their ain't no one in the privy. What made you think there was a man in there?"

"There *was* a man in there," my red-haired wife insisted with some spunk. "I heard him. He shouted, 'Don't shoot me! Don't shoot me!' right into my ear. I leapt out of there so fast I almost tripped over my clothes. Just you give me that there gun and I'll give him what for, scaring me that way!"

"You can have the gun and fire away to your heart's content if you can find him," I told my new bride, handing her the gun. "But I'm telling you, there's no one there."

A WHITEWASHED PRIVY

Jessie snorted in disbelief—not a pretty sound—and stalked back to the privy with the gun cocked. It was empty.

"That's impossible!" My wife said, staring at the empty boards and the two round holes. "I was sitting there," she pointed, "and he spoke right into my ear."

"Maybe you heard someone shouting from the street. The saloon's not too far away," I said.

"Maybe," Jessie said doubtfully. But there really wasn't any other explanation for what she'd heard. Not then.

A few days later I stopped in the privy on my way to work, and someone tried to yank off my drawers while I was answering the call of nature. I felt the yank clearly and saw my pants stretch so far they nearly ripped at the seams. But there weren't nobody in the privy but me. I felt a shiver run down my spine at the sight, and I reached for my pistol, which was in the belt that was scraping across the floor toward the door.

"You stop that right now, you hear?" I shouted gruffly, my hair standing on end. I got my gun untangled and pointed it at the place where my clothes were writhing around. My pants were stuck around my boots, and I heard one of the seams tear as the whatever-it-was yanked them over the boots. I fired my gun at the spot where a person would be if he were messing with my clothes. The bullet splintered the door of the privy, and the yanking stopped at once.

"Don't shoot me," a man's voice called hoarsely from the air in front of my boots. "Don't shoot me!" The temperature around me plummeted, and I could see my breath frosting in midair. The thing gave a wail that seemed to rise up through the roof of the privy. Then it was gone.

I gulped, finished my business real quick, and leapt out of the whitewashed privy as fast as I could. That no-good accountant had sold me a haunted privy! If I ever tracked him down, I'd make him dance the Texas two-step with my pistol. It took me a few minutes to regain my self-control.

Once I was calm, I walked to the mercantile and opened the store for the day. Someone in town knew all about my privy, I was sure of that. And that someone would probably stop in my mercantile sometime or other to buy food or dry goods. I just had to wait, and ask questions of everyone who came in. Sooner or later I'd find out all the things that no-good accountant hadn't told me when he made the sale.

To my surprise my information came two days later, and it came from the local Catholic priest. We got to chatting as I sold him a barrel of white flour and some fishhooks, and I gave him my standard line about wanting to know more about the house I'd just bought from a local accountant. The priest gave me a startled look, and then his eyes narrowed some.

"Having some problems with the plumbing?" he asked casually.

"Our pump is just fine," I said cautiously. "But our privy could use some work."

"Ah!" the priest exclaimed knowingly. He glanced around the store. Finding himself the only occupant, he leaned on the counter and told me the following story.

It seemed a miner named James McKenna had formed a partnership with four other fellows and put himself in charge of the treasury. McKenna was a member of the priest's congregation and did a fine job acting holy . . . on Sundays. But during the week it seemed he had his hand in the company till. One cold winter day McKenna did a runner with all the cash in the cash box. But he weren't too smart about it. Instead of busting outta town, he meandered up the street to the local saloon, where he bought some drinks and flirted with one of the madams who worked there.

Unfortunately for McKenna his partners tracked him down pretty quick. They found him and the madam in an upstairs room, and McKenna fled the premises in a rather disheveled state, slipping and sliding among the snowbanks as he ran. He dodged his pursuers by slipping into a whitewashed privy down by the creek. But one of them saw him sneaking into the building, and the partners decided to teach the little sneak a lesson before discharging him from his duties. They lay in wait at the corner of the street and shot into the air above McKenna's head every time he opened the privy door. After a couple of hours of this entertainment, the businessmen decided they'd had enough of the sport and went home, figuring McKenna would abandon the privy once he saw the coast was clear. But McKenna, afraid for his life, huddled the rest of that night in a corner of the privy and slowly froze to death.

"They say his ghost still haunts that privy," the priest said in conclusion of his tale. "The accountant used to hear him begging his partners not to shoot. And sometimes the ghost played tricks on the accountant, stealing his clothes, saying rude things, laughing in his ear. Sometimes he even sings—which is a real shame because McKenna couldn't hold a tune to save his life."

The priest gave a sigh. "The accountant asked me if I could do something about the spirit, but exorcism isn't my specialty, and none of the prayers I said over the place ever worked."

"Well," I said slowly. "At least that explains why he sold out at such a low price."

The priest departed with his flour barrel and fishhooks, and I spent the rest of the day wondering if I should tell Jessie our privy was haunted. I didn't want to scare her, and the ghost sounded harmless enough. When I got home for dinner, it became immediately apparent that Jessie already knew about the haunting.

"That . . . that . . . that horrible invisible man was back in the privy again this afternoon," Jessie sputtered as she viciously chopped the fresh vegetables she'd brought in from our garden. "He propositioned me as if I was one of the girls in the saloon down the street! I gave him what for and boxed the place I assumed his ears were supposed to be, but he just laughed and kept making rude comments until I finished in there. Next time I go, I'm taking a gun with me!"

I gazed admiringly at my red-cheeked wife. That spunky spirit was why I married her. Well, that and her good looks . . . and her apple pie. I unstrapped one of my guns and laid it on the kitchen table beside the vegetables. She nodded her thanks and kept chopping.

The next few weeks weren't too pleasant—at least they weren't in the privy department, if you catch my drift. McKenna's ghost didn't always appear when we used the privy. He'd stay quiet for days and then break out afresh with terrible screams of "Don't shoot me!" He was always propositioning my wife, which made Jessie hop up and down with rage. She took to shooting her gun into the air whenever she heard the ghost start talking, which was an effective way of silencing him. But I had to keep plugging all them bullet holes in the roof, or the privy would get a might too airy come winter.

McKenna wasn't so nice to me. I had to keep one hand on my britches at all times or he'd try to steal them. And he'd cuss me out something awful, when he wasn't making nasty remarks about my physical appearance.

The last straw for me came late one evening when we'd been enjoying a few days respite from the spirit. I went to use the privy just before bed, and that son of a gun locked me in. As I cussed and rattled the door handle, that derned ghost started singing bawdy songs in the worst tenor voice I'd ever heard. I kept rattling and cussing, and he kept singing. I swore that if ever I got outta that mess I'd keep my gun handy at all times, even when I went to the privy—especially when I went to the privy! I knew Jessie'd miss me sooner or later and would come to the rescue. I just hoped she'd get here before the ghost drove me plumb loco.

It was after midnight when I heard Jessie's voice outside the door. She told me later that she could hear the ghost singing as soon as she left the house. She yanked and yanked on that door, but it wouldn't open. So she ran back to the house for the gun and shot a bullet into the air above the privy (she didn't want to risk hitting me). I was pushing against the door when she fired the shot, and it opened so fast I went tumbling head over heels. As soon as I righted myself, I told Jessie we were moving in the morning. And that's just what we did.

I sold the mercantile, and we moved down to Denver to be closer to Jessie's folks. The very next year, Central City burned to the ground, and the whitewashed privy burnt along with it. But McKenna's ghost kept right on haunting. No privy in that section of town was safe from his pranks and his singing, and he made things very uncomfortable, especially for the ladies. Jessie and I agreed that we got out of Central City just in time!

2

A Friendly Game of Cards

JULESBURG

A storm was already brewing on the horizon when Mr. Brown, the "proprietor" of the tent store–cum–gambling establishment pitched near the brand-new railroad depot in Julesburg, packed up his store goods, and set up the gambling tables.

"Looks like we're in for some stormy weather," a miner fresh down from the hills remarked, spitting tobacco out of the door of the tent in deference to his host. "Them clouds has twisters in them, mark my words."

"They can twist all they want, just so long as they don't interrupt my card game," said the Professor, a seller of patent medicines who traveled up and down the railroad, promising miracles to whoever needed them (and also to many who didn't).

Soon a friendly game of cards was underway. As the evening progressed and the men began nipping out of the Professor's patent medicine bottle, Mr. Brown started winning. He won a pair of mules from a man running a supply wagon, and then he won the wagon that went with them. He won a case of patent medicine from the Professor and an entire poke of gold from one of the miners who periodically drifted in and out of his establishment. Being a sporting man—as well as a clever store

10

proprietor—he lost just enough hands to keep his fellow players in the game.

The Wagoner had just won back one of his mules when the threatened storm came crashing down on the big Army-issue tent. Rain lashed fiercely down on the roof, making it sink down toward the heads of the gamblers, but they played on. Lightning lit the sky and thunder rumbled grandly, as if the gods themselves were playing ninepin in the sky. The Professor won back two of his medicine bottles, and Mr. Brown won the watch off the wrist of a freighter who worked for the railroad.

All at once there came a vivid strike of lightning, followed by a huge crash of thunder. Wind smashed into the tent, making the sides flap wildly about like the sails of an unmanned ship. But the tent was sturdy, and the stakes held it in place. Then suddenly, out of nowhere, a man appeared in the doorway.

The gamblers peered at him in the glimmering lantern light. He was a well set-up man of perhaps forty with a full head of black hair, wicked black eyes, and a mustache that was the instant envy of every man in the tent. He bore himself with a confidence that bordered on bravado, and when he smiled, his teeth gleamed. The man swaggered into the tent and dropped his hat on the table across from Mr. Brown. "Name's Pierce," he drawled. "Do you have room for another?"

"Do you have money?" asked Mr. Brown, eyeing the new victim intently. Pierce drew a wad out of the inner pocket of his coat, and the eyes of every man at the poker table grew intent. Only the Professor seemed uneasy at the appearance of this new player. The patent-medicine man kept looking at the man's hat and coat. There was no earthly way the man could have gotten into the tent without being soaked by the heavy rain, but the stranger's hat and coat were completely dry. The Professor felt his skin crawl, and he was glad Mr. Brown had dealt him out of the next hand.

He settled himself in a corner and pretended to doze in his chair as the next several rounds of poker took place. He was not surprised to see the "friendly" game of cards turn unfriendly mighty quick. As the rain beat down on the tent and the thunder roared across the sky, the new fellow, Pierce, started to win. He won the first pot. He won the second. He won the mules and wagon off Mr. Brown and the watch and poke of gold, too. He sat with his back to the tent door, the lightning occasionally silhouetting his trim form, and he smiled with his perfect white teeth as he once more he laid down a winning hand—this time a full house with three aces. The Professor's eyes narrowed. Always, there were aces—aces in every hand that Pierce won. The man was cheating. He had to be. But watch as he might, the Professor could not see how.

Mr. Brown had cottoned onto it, too. He suddenly leapt to his feet, shouting: "Cheater!"

"Now hold on Brown," said the miner, catching him by the shoulder as he lunged across the table. "If he's cheating, I can't see how. Unless he's a magician."

"Three aces," hissed Mr. Brown. "Again. He always has aces and kings."

"No man is that lucky," said the Professor from his corner, no longer feigning sleep. "Let's see what the cards say."

He grabbed the remaining hand on the table and flipped through it. Sure enough, there were three more aces there, exactly matching the ones in Pierce's full house. With shouts of rage, the miner and the freighter tried to jump Pierce. A scuffle

A FRIENDLY GAME OF CARDS

ensued, making the tent shake and the lanterns flicker. Somehow Pierce remained untouched. Red with anger, Mr. Brown pulled a gun. And before the Professor could stop him, he shot Pierce point-blank in the chest. Pierce grabbed his heart. It was a dramatic gesture, more theater than pain, the Professor noted with the small part of his mind that wasn't transfixed with the horror of the moment. Then Pierce grinned evilly at Mr. Brown and reached across the table toward the store proprietor, his hands dripping blood over everything. And then he vanished.

Outside the tent a bolt of lightning struck a nearby tree, setting it on fire, and above their heads a clap of thunder shook the ground. The gamblers stared in shock at the place where Pierce had been but a moment before. It was empty. But they could still see the drops of blood that drew a shaky line from the back of the chair, across the table, and over the three aces in Pierce's cheating hand of cards. Suddenly a gust of wind came in the door and crashed around inside the tent, making the lanterns swing. Pierce's cards swirled up in the sudden whirlwind, twisting around and around like a miniature tornado.

Out of thin air a phantom voice—Pierce's voice—began to laugh. The laughter grew louder and more manic with every passing second. The gamblers clapped their hands to their ears to shield them, but the laughter went on and on. Then all at once the whirlwind of cards sailed out through the flapping door of the tent, and the laughter followed it. Both disappeared into the raging storm.

With a terrible scream Mr. Brown raced through a door in the back, abandoning the tent, his winnings, and all the goods he sold in his store. He was never seen in Julesburg again.

3

Dunraven

ESTES PARK

I stood gawking in astonishment at the snow-covered mountain peaks that surrounded the Stanley Hotel while my husband patiently juggled our luggage. There were pillars at the edge of the front courtyard, and they added a stately touch to the amazing view.

"Come on, honey. This luggage is getting heavy," my husband called to me. With a sigh of delight, I picked up my suitcase and turned to face the elegant neoclassical four-story hotel. The roof was red and a small tower rose from the middle of the building, directly over the elegantly pillared front porch. I smiled and followed my husband up the main staircase.

I had been as excited as a child when I learned we would be spending a weekend in the Stanley Hotel. The hotel had been the inspiration for Stephen King's book *The Shining*, and it was rumored to be haunted by more than one ghost! The ghost tours were completely booked for today, but we'd signed up to take one tomorrow, after our hike in the Rocky Mountain National Park. A ghost tour sounded like fun, though of course I didn't believe in ghosts myself.

We entered the elegant lobby, and I drifted over to look at the Stanley Steamer parked just inside the front door while my husband checked us in. F. O. Stanley, the original owner of the hotel, was the coinventor of the Stanley Steamer, and somehow the antique car fit right in with the decor. I turned away from the car and studied my surroundings thoughtfully, taking in the beamed ceiling, the wood paneling of the walls, the fireplace surrounded by comfortable couches.

Then I caught sight of a tall raffish man with a goatee who was standing on the floor beside the grand staircase, leaning casually against the railing. He was dressed for some sort of fancy party, in a formal—if rather old-fashioned—suit and, good heavens, a cravat! His eyes were merry and a bit wicked, and he stared intently at me for so long that it made me nervous. I felt myself blushing, and I turned back to the vintage Stanley Steamer, uneasy for no reason I could explain. I shivered a bit, feeling his eyes boring into the back of my dress.

Then my husband joined me, saying: "We've got a room on the fourth floor. Let's go."

I nodded, braced myself, and turned toward the staircase, certain the man would still be looking at me. But he had disappeared. Relieved, I picked up my suitcase and started up the stairs, feeling very elegant myself in such surroundings. I was glad I'd worn a nice summer dress today, instead of the jeans I'd originally pulled out of the drawer at home.

We reached the landing and headed up the left staircase toward the second floor. And suddenly, the raffish man was right behind me, walking too close for comfort, his feet hitting the step behind me at the same moment I took the next one. We were only an inch or two apart as we climbed the stairs, and I put on speed as I neared the second-floor hallway. This was getting creepy. I hadn't seen the man at all when we reached the landing. He must have been lurking on the other staircase.

I stepped into the hallway and turned right, hurrying so fast I almost stepped on my husband's heels. When I risked a glance over my shoulder, my stalker had disappeared again.

Perhaps it was just a coincidence, I thought. He might be one of those men who have no instinct for personal space. Still, it had been an unpleasant experience. I shuddered and dogged my husband's steps up the third- and the fourth-floor staircases, glancing over my shoulder now and then to make sure the man wasn't following us. Each time I looked, there was no one there. By the time we reached the door of 401, I was feeling a bit foolish. It must have been a coincidence!

After unpacking and using the bathroom, we hurried downstairs, eager to explore the town. As we descended the main staircase, I kept a sharp lookout for the gentleman, but he was nowhere to be seen. *Thank goodness.* As we crossed the lobby toward the front doors, I heard music coming from a parlor on our left—classical music. *How very stylish of the hotel to provide us with live music at this hour,* I thought as we exited into the bright summer sunshine.

There was so much to see and do in Estes Park that we didn't get back until quite late. "We'll have to eat at the hotel restaurant tomorrow night," my husband said, nodding toward the corner of the lobby where the unmistakable clink of silverware could be heard. I nodded happily. Folks in town said that the food at the hotel was quite good, and a woman in one of the shops had recommended the steak.

17

As we started up the stairs to our room, I caught a glimpse of a figure standing in the shadows under the staircase. Goose bumps broke out over my arms, and I clutched my husband's arm. He looked at me curiously. "Are you all right, honey?" he asked as we reached the landing and turned to mount the steps to the second floor. "Fine," I replied. I hadn't mentioned the stranger to my husband, since I wasn't sure he was really stalking me. Still, no use taking chances. As we walked down the hallway, I told my husband about the way the man had stared at me in the lobby and then followed me so intimately up the staircase on our arrival. My husband was none too pleased. "I didn't see him," he confessed. "Too wrapped up in getting our luggage upstairs, I guess. What did he look like?"

"He's a tall raffish fellow with a goatee and a wicked twinkle in his eyes. You know, one of those older gents who dresses too fancy for the occasion. He even wore a cravat, if you can believe it," I said. "I bet he pinches the housemaids every chance he can get."

"Sounds like it," my husband said darkly. "If you see him again, point him out to me. I'll make sure he backs off."

Relieved, I put the man out of my mind, and we chatted about our agenda for the morrow as we changed for bed. I picked up my small suitcase and carried it over to the closet. As I leaned inside, I felt someone pinch me in the derriere. "Stop that, honey," I said, swatting laughingly at his hand. I missed him completely, my hand sweeping uselessly through thin air. I turned in time to see my husband walking out of the bathroom.

"Stop what?" he asked me.

My eyes widened. "Didn't you pinch me just now?" I asked, the hairs on my neck rising.

DUNRAVEN

"Nope," my husband said with a grin. "Want me to?" he added, leering at me suggestively. One thing led to another after that, and I forgot all about the pinch as we settled down to sleep.

I woke suddenly, my heart pounding with fear, in total darkness. A glance at the bedside clock told me it was 1 a.m. My body was shaking with cold, but I was sweating. It was a strange sensation. My eyes swept the room, as I wondered what had wakened me. And then I saw the man standing at the foot of the bed. He was tall and still smartly dressed with wicked eyes and a goatee, and he was glowing faintly with his own inner light. The man gazed right at me, and I had the clear sense that he wanted to strip off my nightgown and have his way with me. I shrieked in fear and clutched at my husband. He rolled over, waking at once, and saw the shining man at the foot of the bed. *"What in God's name?"* he shouted, sitting bolt upright. Instantly, the man vanished.

I was sobbing uncontrollably, shudders running up and down my body. "Get me out of here," I gasped between sobs. "Right now! I'm not staying here another minute with that wicked old . . . .*phantom.*"

"Right," my husband said. "You stay in that bed and don't move!" He snapped on the light, raced to the closet, and grabbed our suitcases. Within five minutes, all our belongings were crammed into our suitcases and we were heading down four flights of stairs to the lobby.

As my husband approached the front desk to rouse the staff and hand in our key, I glanced nervously around for the raffish ghost with the goatee. My eye lighted on a huge portrait at the far end of the lobby, and I gave a shriek that brought my husband over in a hurry. "That's him," I cried, pointing at the picture. "That's the ghost I saw at the foot of the bed!"

My husband's eyes widened. "That's him all right," he said grimly. He shook his hand at the portrait: "You leave my wife alone, you hear?" he thundered.

The man at the front desk watched us, wide-eyed with astonishment. My husband stalked over to him, handed him our key, and gave him a terse explanation for our sudden departure from the hotel. As soon as the bill was signed, we were out the door and walking through a starry night toward the car park.

"The man at the front desk said he thought our ghost was Lord Dunraven," my husband said grimly, "an English fellow with a reputation for the ladies. He used to own this property before Stanley bought it, and they say his spirit never left."

"His spirit can linger all it wants," I said with a shudder. "I'm leaving!"

And that's just what we did. We drove straight home without stopping, and tumbled into our own bed at about 4 a.m.

We never returned to the Stanley Hotel.

4

Spirit Guide

MANITOU SPRINGS

I believe Mr. Hildebrand, my fiancé, was not pleased that my spirit guide was a man. He never said so, of course, but he became very stiff and formal if I ever mentioned my spirit guide, and I guessed in time the reason why. It was very silly of him. Why should he be jealous of a spirit, even if it was that of a long-dead native warrior who lived somewhere in the western mountains?

Not every spiritualist has a spirit guide, of course. I felt very fortunate to be granted such a blessing. It did not always require a séance to bring my guide to me. Sometimes I heard his voice in my dreams, and sometimes he whispered to me on the wind when I was meditating silently at my window. Only one thing marred my relationship with my spirit guide: I never saw him. Not even in dreams. This saddened me, though I suppose Mr. Hildebrand would have appreciated it if I had ever confided this fact to him. But I did not.

I once asked my mother—a fellow spiritualist with her own spirit guide—if she ever saw the face of the one who instructed her. She laughed mysteriously and would only say, "Perhaps."

Mr. Hildebrand and I were due to be married in the summer, but late in the winter I fell ill and was very slow to recover. Too slow. The doctor came frequently to check on me, and the diagnosis, when it came, was a blow. Tuberculosis. I locked myself away in my room after the doctor left and wrestled with the knowledge, knowing it was a death sentence. Perhaps not as immediate as an accident, but surely just as fatal in the end. I leaned my head against the window frame, staring sightlessly out at the garden, and wept. After a time a soft breeze caressed my cheek. It felt like a warm hand brushing the hair from my eyes and drying my tears. "Come," I heard a deep male whisper. "Come."

It was my spirit guide; the one who called himself Running Buck. "Come where?" I asked the breeze. "Come to my mountains," the reply came after a long pause.

The mountains! Of course. The doctor had recommended we move at once to the mountains, for the efficacy of the mountain air sometimes had a healing effect on tuberculosis cases like mine. Perhaps this was not a death sentence after all.

"Thank you," I called to my spirit guide. Then I went to unlock my door and let my worried mother inside.

Mr. Hildebrand was upset and horrified when he learned of the serious nature of my illness, and of course he insisted that the wedding be postponed. We found a town called Manitou Springs that had mineral springs that were supposed to be helpful for conditions such as mine. And so my family moved to the mountains. My parting with Mr. Hildebrand was quite melancholy, but I could not help a rise in my spirits as we departed westward on the train. "Come to my mountains," Running Buck had said. And I was on my way.

We settled in Manitou Springs, and my first sight of the mountains was transforming. Red Mountain in particular seemed to call to me. Every time I saw it, I felt as if I had come home, which was ridiculous, since I had never been there before. And yet . . .

Although the disease continued to plague me, the mountain air helped my condition. I was less confined to my room and was able to get some light exercise every day, deeply breathing the crisp air. Always, I looked to Red Mountain for comfort. And that was where I first saw him. Tall, proud, with a hawk nose and dark hair to his waist, he stood in the shadow of the mountain and gazed at me with a fierce possessiveness that brought the blood stinging into my cheeks. He was dressed in the simple clothes of a warrior, and he had eagle feathers braided into his hair. It was Running Buck.

I could see him clearly for a moment, and then a ray of sun burst through the leaves overhead, shining right through his body. In an instant he was gone. I sat down heavily on a nearby bench, as breathless as if I had been running. I wanted to meditate on my experience, on what it might mean. But at that moment, I heard Mr. Hildebrand's voice drifting from the front porch, and I knew that my solitary reverie would be interrupted. I felt a pang of irritation. I did not want to talk to Mr. Hildebrand. I wanted to dream about Running Buck. With a sigh I pasted a welcoming smile on my lips as my fiancé came into the garden to greet me.

We held a séance at our house that evening, and our guests were delighted by the ghostly rapping and the messages given to them through my mother's spirit guide. I stayed silent, listening to the others gasp and whisper, my hands held tightly by my fiancé on one side and by my mother on the other.

SPIRIT GUIDE

As the candles burned low, I heard a voice—*his* voice—in my ear. "Come to my mountain. Come to me!" I knew at once I would go.

It was nearly a week before I could get away. My mother strictly monitored my exercise and made me rest more often than I felt was necessary. But one day she departed with a large list of errands and visits she was obliged to make and left me home alone. This was my chance. Running Buck had appeared in my dreams every night since I first saw him in the garden, and he was always in the same place: underneath a tall tree at the top of Red Mountain. "I am waiting," he said in my dream. "Come to me."

A wave of emotion—deep, strong, and true—washed over me every time I saw my spirit guide. Such wild, intense feelings made my gentle affection toward Mr. Hildebrand seem sacrilegious. The disparity between my feelings for the two men was enormous.

I tied a scarf over my hair to keep off the chill and started out for the mountain. Within a few hundred feet I saw him. He was standing farther up the slope, beckoning for me to follow him. With a glad cry I hurried off the track and ascended up and up, through the woods toward the peak above. No matter how fast I walked, Running Buck always stayed a few yards ahead of me. It was maddening. We followed a deer trail that meandered this way and that. Somehow I made it over every fallen tree, every large rock, and through the scree that had dropped from the cliffs above. Keeping my eyes fixed on my spirit guide, I felt I could do anything.

When Running Buck stopped at last, he was standing underneath the pine tree I had seen in my dream. He turned then and held out his arms to me, his dark eyes fierce with affection. I ran to him, my arms closing tightly around a body as warm and full of breath as my own. "Soon," he whispered in my ear. "Soon we will be together as we were meant to be."

I floated down the mountain a long time later, leaving my scarf tied to a branch of the pine tree—that glorious pine tree that was now and forever a piece of heaven to me! I arrived home breathless, fatigued, but still glowing. My mother was furious with me, of course, but I didn't care. I told her my spirit guide had summoned me and I had climbed to the top of Red Mountain in answer to that summons. She didn't believe me. No one did, until a couple of boys climbed to the top of the mountain and saw my scarf fluttering there, tied to the pine tree just as I said it would be.

Within days my physical health declined rapidly, as my spiritual health soared. Mr. Hildebrand and I would never marry now. How could we? My heart was given to another. Running Buck was my lover in spirit and in truth, and we would be together soon. I was unable to rise from my bed, and my loved ones hovered nearby, sensing that the end was near. I wanted to laugh. This was not the end. This was just the beginning. I begged them to bury me at the top of Red Mountain, underneath the tree where I had tied my scarf. The place where Running Buck and I had first embraced. I had not seen my spirit guide since I left the mountaintop, but I sensed his presence beside me, helping me bear the pain as my body and soul prepared for a final sundering. At the end, my vision darkened, and I was walking through a long tunnel. For a moment I was frightened. Where was Running Buck? Then a light appeared ahead of me. I hurried toward it, feeling as light and swift on my feet as a child. I stepped onto the slope of Red Mountain and saw my handsome warrior standing before me with an incandescent smile on his face and love in his eyes. He embraced me fiercely, and then we grabbed hands like two courting children and ran up to the very top of Red Mountain. Our spirits kept going, up and up as the world dropped away from us, leaving us in a heaven of our own making.

Sometimes . . . yes, sometimes we drop back to Earth—to the old pine tree where we first embraced. If we see a person we know—a spiritualist or someone from town—we smile at them and hold hands. Some of them see us—I know my mother did when she visited my grave under the pine tree. I think it comforts her to know how happy I am.

5

Dead Man's Canyon

NEAR COLORADO SPRINGS

I whistled cheerfully as I left the lawyer's office with an official document in my hand that said I was the new owner of a ranch. I'd been working hard for the last several years as a cowboy, but I'd grown tired of wrangling cattle for someone else. I wanted to wrangle my own cattle, and I'd saved enough now to buy me a small herd to go on my new ranch.

I hurried to the bank and put my copy of the deed in a safe deposit box. Then I jumped on my horse and headed out of town. It was a bit late to start for Colorado Springs, but I was too excited to care. I meant to propose to my gal just as soon as I reached her house. We'd waited long enough, and I didn't aim to wait a minute longer! My horse felt my excitement and started dancing around. I let him go for a few minutes to wear us both out a bit. Then we settled into the jog that we used out on the trail, one that we could keep up all day.

As we headed east, the cool breeze off the mountain and the gentle murmuring of the creek calmed me down. I loved being outdoors. No desk job for me. No sir. Sitting inside four walls all day long would drive me mad inside a month. I heard a raven cawing overhead, saw him catch the breeze and soar up and up. Closer to earth, the smaller birds were chirping and twittering and flitting through the trees. My horse gave a funny sort of huff underneath me; his version of a happy sigh. I couldn't blame him. I eased off, and we settled into a gentle walk, enjoying the late afternoon together.

As the miles passed, my thoughts gradually shifted from rosy dreams of me and my gal living on the new ranch to a sharper awareness of the trail ahead. The sun was sinking fast behind Blue Mountain, and dusk was no time to be riding through Dead Man's Canyon. Yet here I was, more fool me, doing just that. Of course I didn't believe in ghosts. That was just foolishness. But you heard stories . . .

It started with a murder about ten, fifteen years ago. A man named Harkins was found dead outside his cabin. He'd been killed with an ax, and that ax was still buried deep in his forehead when he was found. The murderers had stolen his white horse and robbed his homestead. They were later brought to justice, but this had done nothing to appease Harkins, at least that's what the storytellers said.

A few years back a traveler walking this path from Cañon City to Colorado Springs was confronted by a bearded man at dusk. At first glance the man looked like he was wearing a strange hat. Then the traveler realized that what looked like a hat was really an ax sticking obscenely out of his forehead. It was the ghost of Harkins, returned to the place where his homestead once stood. And he was angry! The phantom came straight for the traveler, arms outstretched to grab him. The traveler's horse spooked and threw him into the creek, but that phantom kept coming.

The traveler jumped up lickety-split and ran for it, screaming bloody murder. A couple of riders on the same trail came galloping up to see what was wrong and saw the ghost knock the poor traveler head over heels. The riders started shooting, thinking the ghost was a highwayman. Then they saw the ax in his forehead and panicked, their shots going every which way as they tried to get away from the ghost. In the melee, one of the horses was injured, one of the riders shot his own foot, and the ghost disappeared.

When things had calmed down a mite, the poor traveler crawled out of the rocks where he'd landed when the ghost knocked him over and promptly fainted at the feet of his rescuers. He didn't wake up till he was safe in the doctor's house.

Chills ran up my arms as I recalled this story. I shuddered slightly, my eyes scanning the cottonwoods by the stream, the pine and juniper trees on the ridge. There was nothing to be seen, not even a bird. We were alone on the trail, my horse and I. The creek babbled softly nearby, and my horse's hoofbeats were loud in my ears as the sky changed from light blue to dark blue to deep indigo.

It was getting real dark in the mountains' shadow. It would be night soon. I wanted out of Dead Man's Canyon before then. I urged my horse back into our working jog. Obediently he picked up his pace. Then he tossed his head and froze in place. Years of experience kept me in the saddle, but it was a close thing. I whipped out my gun and followed my horse's gaze. Was it rustlers? Highwaymen? (A *ghost,* my treacherous inner thoughts whispered.)

The wind whipped off the ridge, biting cold as it howled down from the snow line. My teeth began to chatter, but I kept my gun hand still, finger on the trigger.

DEAD MAN'S CANYON

And then it came for me, a misty white figure whipping out from the bushes and traveling fast. It solidified before my eyes into the glowing figure of a bearded man with an ax sticking sickeningly from his forehead. Silvery blood gushed down from the wound. Light poured around us like some ghastly parody of sunrise. Beneath me my horse screamed, reared, bolted. I clung on with one hand and got off a couple of wild shots as my horse fled from the phantom.

After a moment, the apparition disappeared, plunging us instantly into darkness. The ghastly light of the ghost had ruined my night vision, and I bent double along my horse's neck, afraid a low-hanging branch might sweep me off. We were in the cottonwoods now, and then thundering across the creek. That's when the ghost reappeared, materializing right in front of us in a blaze of blue light. He was laughing maniacally and waved his arms in my horse's face. My horse screamed and shied. I nearly pitched off as my horse backed away on his hind legs, kicking out at the horrible phantom with his front feet. Then he whirled and raced back through the creek and up onto the path. The phantom followed us at a supernaturally fast pace, running first on one side, then the other. He was driving us like we drove cattle.

I was gasping with terror, sweat pouring off me as I clung onto the reins for dear life. But somewhere in my hindbrain, a little piece of me was getting mad. How dare he treat us like cattle?

The phantom swerved again, driving us to the left. And suddenly we were in a dead-end passage with no way out. My horse reared when he found his path blocked by sheer stone walls and whirled with a third scream of terror to face our tormenter. He was on his hind legs again, kicking out at the floating phantom with the obscenely gory ax in its forehead.

"Right. I've had enough," I said grimly to my horse. I fired my gun right into the ghost until I was out of bullets. Then I kneed my horse, bringing him down on all fours. We'd worked together for a lot of years, my horse and I, and I swear he could read my thoughts. "We're going through," I shouted, giving him an encouraging nudge. He hesitated for a fraction of a second, and then he obeyed. We rode straight at the ghost, and suddenly the phantom wasn't laughing. Then we were riding right through his glowing figure. For a moment it felt as if my body and spirit were tangling up with his. Piercing cold shot through me like icy knives, making my lungs heave and strain. My skull felt as if it were tearing open under a massive blow. All I could see was blinding white light. All I could feel was pain.

And then we were through, and my horse was galloping madly up the dark trail, heedless of the darkness, the trees, the rocky hillside. He leapt a boulder easily and kept going. I clung on in a daze. We seemed to have left the ghost behind us. There was no more blue light—just immense, terrible darkness and a throbbing pain in my head. Instinct kept me in the saddle, even though my body was shivering so bad my teeth rattled. Sweat was pouring down my face, into my eyes, blinding me. I fumbled my gun into the holster and wiped the sweat out of my eyes. My fingers came away dark. It was blood, not sweat. We came into an open stretch, and my horse, no longer pursued, slowed his frantic pace, sides heaving mightily. I touched my throbbing forehead and felt blood gushing from a wound up there. I swayed in the saddle and almost slipped off. But I caught myself and lay slowly down along my horse's neck, clinging to his mane.

"Take me to Judith, boy," I gasped to him, hoping he'd read my mind like he had often done when we were wrangling a herd of stampeding cattle. And he did. I must have lost consciousness, because my next memory was of Judith's voice exclaiming in alarm and her father's hands pulling me off my horse and helping me into the house. They called the doc and he came and stitched my skull, teasing me for running into a tree. I didn't correct him. I didn't want him thinking I was mad or a drunk. I did tell Judith and her pa what happened though, once the doctor was gone. And before I went to bed that night, I took a good long look in the mirror. Sure enough, the gash on my forehead was in the exact place where the ax blow had killed Harkins.

It was Judith who summed up the story for me in one emphatic sentence. "Honey," she said to me as she bade me goodnight. "From now on, we're taking the long way around."

You said it, darlin'.

6

Rented Rooms

DENVER

His business took him to Denver often, and he grew to love the city in the shadow of the Rocky Mountains. After his latest transaction came to an end, he began seeking rooms in the vicinity of the business district, hoping himself to become a resident of the fair city. After many days of searching, an advertisement led him to a small two-storied cottage off a side street. It was almost rural in its setting, and it attracted him at once.

When the businessman knocked on the door, an elderly woman answered and agreed to show him the rooms for let. She was a sweet grandmotherly type with a slightly worried air, and he found her pleasant and well-spoken. She took him upstairs to the two-room apartment, and he was pleased to see that the front room overlooked the garden. It was comfortably furnished as a sitting room, with a nice fireplace, chairs, a sofa, and a writing desk. The floor-length windows at the front gave onto a second-story veranda where he could sit in the evenings and enjoy the sunset over the mountains to the west. He turned then to the second room, which was connected to the first via a door in the center of the wall. Inside this spacious room was a large bed, a table with a washbasin and water jug, and a wardrobe. It was by far the nicest apartment he had seen in the city, and the businessman took it at once, paying two months' rent in advance for the lovely rooms. Then he went to fetch his luggage from the hotel where he was staying.

After unpacking his belongings, the businessman went to a nearby boardinghouse for dinner and then settled himself before the cozy fire in the front room to read before retiring to bed. Engrossed in his book, two hours passed away before he became aware that he was no longer alone in the room. The sensation of a presence was overwhelming, and he looked up, expecting to see his new landlady framed in the hall doorway. No one was there. His skin prickled, and he gave a little shiver. The sensation of someone watching him was still there. He glanced around the room, then got up, leaving his book open on the chair, and carried the oil lamp around both his new rooms, checking the fastenings of every door and every window and looking into every shadowy nook. He tugged the curtains shut, thinking that he must have sensed the gaze of someone passing on the street below. Satisfied that he was truly alone, the businessman went back to his chair to continue reading.

He hadn't been seated for very long when he felt the presence again. This time it was accompanied by the distinct rustle of a woman's dress. He looked up sharply. For a moment he thought he saw the outline of a woman disappearing through the wall between the front room and the hallway. He gasped, the book slipping out of his suddenly sweaty hands. It hit the floor with a bang, making him jump. His heart pounded heavily against his ribs, and he fought to control his breathing. It was only a shadow, he told himself. Only a shadow.

Retrieving his book from the floor, he tried to read, but his gaze kept returning to the opposite wall. His thoughts kept swerving back to the shadow he'd seen. Had it been real? Of course not. And yet . . .

Scolding himself for believing such superstitious nonsense, he picked up the lantern and headed into the bedroom. At the last minute he shut the door and bolted it, feeling foolish for doing so. Then he undressed and slipped into the very comfortable bed. He turned to blow at the lantern and then hesitated, remembering the shadow. He decided to turn the wick down as low as it would go, and then he lay looking at the dancing shadows on the wall until he fell into a fitful slumber.

He was awakened suddenly by the sensation of a clammy hand brushing across his face. He rose halfway with a gasp and saw a shadowy shape standing beside his bed. He could see the light of the lantern shining directly through its translucent form. He stared at the vague outline before him, his body frozen in fear. As he watched with bulging eyes, the form drifted backward through the wood of the door and vanished into the front room. With a muffled shriek, he fell back against the pillows, his heart hammering in his chest. After taking several deep breaths, he rubbed his eyes and sat up again. The room was empty. Had he dreamed the figure? Or was it real? He picked up the lantern with shaking hands and went to examine the door. It was bolted shut.

"It must have been a dream," he muttered, getting back into bed and placing the lantern on the bedside table. He tossed and turned for more than an hour, watching the level of the oil in the lantern as it slowly burned. When the lamp guttered out, he sighed, turned over, and went to sleep.

He came awake a second time with a feeling of such dread that he pressed his hands fiercely into the mattress, hanging on for dear life as if he were in a storm-tossed ship. Ghastly white light spilled from the open door to the front room. Around him the air was so cold his breath came out in a mist that hovered above his face. Reluctantly he turned his gaze toward the light, and in horror he watched the towering figure of a man in evening dress dragging a lovely young woman in a white dress across the floor of the front room by her hair. The vision was enacted in complete silence, which in a strange way terrified him more than if he could have heard them. The man's face was twisted in a grotesque rictus of anger, and the woman was screaming silently, kicking her feet against the floor, her hands desperately gripping at the floorboards. The woman's long nails scraped into the wood, leaving long lines behind as she was dragged through the open door into the bedroom. Flinging her from him, the glowing man groped in the drawer of the bedside table and pulled out a glittering knife. Lunging forward, he grabbed the woman by the hair once again and slit her throat so hard he almost severed her head from her body. The silence was broken then by a ghastly shriek from the ghost's victim as hot red blood splashed down upon her white dress. The sound ripped through the businessman's nerves like the knife had ripped through her throat. Her body fell to the floor with a crash that shook the room. It felt as if the whole cottage was caving in. The businessman's eyes rolled back in his head and he fainted, slumping back against the bed.

When the man woke, bright sunshine was streaming through the window. He gazed sightlessly at it, seeing an inner vision of a glowing phantom with a glittering knife, hearing

RENTED ROOMS

a ghastly shriek. He leapt up suddenly, dressing with shaking hands and throwing his clothes willy-nilly into his suitcase. He was crossing the room when he caught sight of himself in the mirror and stopped in horror. Overnight his black hair had turned completely white!

With a gasp the businessman tore his gaze from the mirror, unbolted the bedroom door, and tottered with trembling legs into the front room where he'd first seen the white light. The room looked completely normal, with the sunlight lighting up the closed curtains and the fire burnt away to ashes. Even his book still lay open on the chair. And then he saw that the pages of the book were splattered with blood. With a cry of horror, he grabbed up his suitcase and left the house at a run, never to return.

About a year after his abrupt departure, the businessman heard that the cottage was slated for demolition. Some morbid curiosity brought him to the property on his lunch hour to watch the men at work. The front wall was already off the house, and he could see the fireplace of his former sitting room through the gap. The men were tearing enthusiastically into the wall beside it when they made a gruesome discovery. A bricked-up closet lay behind that wall, and a woman's skeleton was bundled into the bottom of it. The rotting remains of her white dress were still stained red with blood.

7

Empty Bucket

LEADVILLE

When he asked for work at the Morning Star Mine, the supervisor gave him a strange look before hiring him. He was new to this country, so he wasn't sure what the supervisor's look meant. Everything in this land was strange to him. Perhaps all new hires were given such a thoughtful, penetrating stare before they were taken on. But it seemed to Dieter as if the supervisor was plotting something. Nonsense, of course. Still, he determined to be cautious down there in the mine.

He went at once to report for duty, and one of the men took him to the supply room to outfit him for the job. Pickax, dynamite, shovel, hard hat, lantern, and other paraphernalia were assigned to him, and he had to sign for it all in a book. The man seemed friendly enough, but his hands were shaking as he fumbled with the pages of the book. "Sign here," he said gruffly to Dieter. Dieter eyed the man warily and then signed his name. Something wasn't right here. First the supervisor, now this man. What, he wondered, had happened down there?

The man walked him to the entrance of the mine, and two men came to work the windlass. Dieter lit his lantern and stepped into the bucket. The men at the windlass nodded gruffly to him and then looked away quickly. They did not appear happy at all as they began lowering him into the mine.

After a few moments' descent, the light from above dimmed, and Dieter was in darkness save for the flickering of the lantern in his hand. He stared hard at the walls as they passed, wondering if he had correctly interpreted the body language of the miners at the windlass and of the man who'd fitted him out. The man with the book had hunched his shoulders in fear when Dieter told him the drift to which he'd been assigned.

Dieter shivered, and the movement made the lantern light flicker off the walls. The shadows bounced menacingly around the bucket, and his own shadow looked more like that of a beast than a man. When the bucket hit bottom, he gave a little cry, startled by the sudden jolt and the shadows that jumped at him from every wall. Instantly he felt ashamed. He was an experienced miner; he should not be shying at shadows. He squared his shoulders and stepped out of the bucket.

Drawing in a deep breath, Dieter turned slowly around, taking in his surroundings. Outside the lantern light, the mine was pitch-black. Above him the merest pinprick of light revealed the entrance. The air in the mine was damp and felt rather stale, as if no one had been down there in quite some time. Water was trickling from somewhere. It sounded as if an underground stream was flowing somewhere in the shaft. A cold drop fell onto his neck, and he shivered as it ran underneath his collar like a spectral finger running down his spine.

In his second visual circuit of the mine, Dieter's eye was caught by a newly cleared space at the far end of the shaft, probably the site of the last blast. It did not look as if it had been cleaned up properly. He frowned disapprovingly. That was no way to run a mine. He shouldered his pickax and took a step forward. And then he stopped abruptly. Something had caught his eye when he swung the lantern toward the end of the shaft— something that shouldn't be there.

His pulses throbbed with superstitious fear as he slowly turned the lantern, looking around. Then he saw a man's boot sticking out from behind an outcropping of rock, and his heart started slamming against his ribs, taking away his breath. His hands were icy cold, and he almost dropped the lantern as he went into the shadows and turned over the body of a man—a dead man. At least Dieter hoped he was dead. No one living should have such a terrible dent in the top of his head. One side of the man's pale face was completely caved in. The undamaged side had a scar running from eyebrow to ear, disappearing inside the man's ruddy beard.

"*Mein Gott,*" Dieter gasped, dropping the body back into the shadows. For a moment his stomach lurched and he thought he would be sick. He fought for control, and finally his will overrode his sensibilities. Straightening, he ran to the bucket and started shaking the ropes. "*Hilfe! Hilfe!*" he shouted for help at the top of his lungs, hoping the sound would reach the men at the top.

After a long moment the men shouted down to him, asking him what was wrong.

"There is a dead man here," he shouted back. "Fell down the shaft, he did, and his head hit upon a stone. What should I do?"

There was silence above while the men conferred. Then they told him to put the dead man into the bucket, and they would haul him up. Dieter grimaced in distaste for this task, but it was the only humane thing to do for the dead man, so he dragged

EMPTY BUCKET

the heavy body over and dumped it into the bucket. After a moment the ropes tightened and the bucket and its grisly cargo began to rise. Dieter turned away, his duty done, and hurriedly picked up the lantern. He headed down to the drift to begin the day's work.

The work steadied him. It was hard, but he had done harder work in the past. He drilled one hole, then another and another, preparing the site for another blast. It would be easier with two men to drill, but perhaps the supervisor would hire someone else before the day was done. He had almost forgotten about the dead man by the time he was ready to quit for the day. He went back to the entrance, hoping the other men had sent the bucket back down for him. Yes, it was there. He stepped inside and signaled for the others to bring him up. As the walls began to move around him, he wondered if they had identified the man who had fallen to his death in the mine. He hoped so, for the family's sake.

He had no sooner stepped out of the bucket than Dieter was accosted by one of his fellow miners. "What do you mean by that trick you played this morning?!" shouted the man who had fitted him out earlier. "There was no dead body in that bucket you sent up! I ought to report you to the supervisor."

"What mean you, no body?" cried Dieter, shocked to the core.

The two men squared off eye to eye, neither giving an inch. They were separated a moment later by the supervisor. "Take it easy," the supervisor said. He turned to Dieter. "Listen, can you describe this corpse you found in the drift?" he asked.

"Certainly," Dieter said. He described the man in detail: height, weight, pale coloring, red beard, and the scar running from his eyebrow to his ear. He even described the terrible wound in the man's head. As Dieter spoke, the supervisor's face went a waxy gray and the man who had fitted him out gasped and sank abruptly to his knees.

"That's Wilson," he whispered to the supervisor. "He found Wilson's body. No wonder it disappeared on the way up the shaft!"

"What mean you?" demanded Dieter sharply. "Explain to me now!"

The supervisor drew in a deep breath and explained. There had been a cave-in in the drift a few days ago. Wilson had been caught in it and killed. His body had been found beneath a pile of rubble with a dent in his skull such as Dieter had described and one side of his face was smashed in.

"*Mein Gott!*" Dieter gasped, his knees giving way. "You mean a ghost it was I put into the bucket?" He sank onto the ground, unable to stand. "*Mein Gott!* A ghost!" He rubbed his hands together, trying to wipe away the feel of the dead man's body. "And *you knew,*" he added accusingly, glaring up at the supervisor. "And so did *you!*" He swung around to point accusingly at his fellow miner. Both men looked away.

"I leave instantly," Dieter said, pushing himself upright. "Not a minute more will I stay here. For my day's work, you will pay me now."

Glumly, the supervisor nodded. He paid Dieter his due and muttered, "We might as well close that drift. No one is going to work there once word of that ghost gets around."

"Sure of that, you may be!" snapped Dieter. And he walked away, never to return.

8

The Piper

TELLURIDE

It is a terrible thing to lose one's lass. Worse still, when a man has slaved in the mines for years to earn enough money to support her, he doesn't want to learn that his lass has thrown him over and married another man. Our wedding date had been set for April 1888, and now it would never happen. I never realized until the moment I read Marie's letter that a broken heart caused real, physical pain. But the bolt of agony that ripped through my gut and tightened every muscle in my chest felt worse than the pain I had when I broke my leg in two places. The whole world went gray around me, and I don't actually remember much from the moment I received the letter until I found myself with my burro on an icy, snow-packed trail about twelve thousand feet up the mountain.

The gusting wind buffeted my burro and me, and its cold slap on my face startled me from my stupor. I stared around at the beautiful, treacherous mountains, trying to get my bearings. Beside me my burro sighed and sat down abruptly in the middle of the trail. She'd been working hard while my mind was elsewhere, and now she refused to take another step along this hazardous trail. Really, I couldn't blame her. I sat down next to her, studying the dizzying scenery around me. It looked as if I'd climbed the saddle that divided Ourey County from San Miguel. So at least I knew where I was. Not that it helped much. It was early spring, and a blizzard might sweep down at any moment, or the packed snow underfoot could give way, sweeping away my burro and me. Somehow I couldn't make myself care much.

I must have left the Virginius Mine without collecting my pay, because when I rummaged around my saddlebags, all I found were some dried beef, beans, coffee, a little bread, and a few measly coins. I turned and looked back at the way I'd come. In the bowl of white snow far below I saw the shaft houses, rough cabins, ugly slag piles newly pulled from the mine, and crisscrossing trails. The sight tightened my heart, as if being squeezed by a big fist. Again the gray came down before my eyes. All that work for my lass, and she'd betrayed me. No, I wouldn't go back for my pay. I grabbed a hunk of bread from a saddlebag and sat down beside my burro again in the icy path. My nether regions would probably freeze, but that didn't seem to matter either.

The sharp wind died away as I ate, leaving behind an eerie silence. I heard nothing but the occasional crackle of ice as it warmed in the sun and the steady breathing of my burro. It would probably be warmer if I sat on a rock outcropping, I mused in the uncanny silence. But I couldn't be bothered. Another wave of gut-wrenching grief suddenly ripped through me, and I gasped, doubling over in pain. I could see my lass's face so clearly. *Oh, Marie.*

And that's when I heard the pipes. The sound startled me so much, I straightened up and then scrambled to my feet. Who on earth would be playing the bagpipes on top of a mountain trail? That was insane. Had he or she never heard of avalanches? Glancing around, I realized that the snowbanks around me looked secure. The pipes played on.

Now I was curious. I followed the sound down the trail, slipping a little. "Piper, show yourself!" I called. No one answered. The tune was a rollicking ballad I remembered from my youth in Scotland, and my toes started tapping to the rhythm. I scrambled on and then remembered my burro and turned back. She'd risen to her feet and was lazily ambling back the way we'd come.

"Oh no you don't," I called, hurrying back to grab her lead. As I did, the piper's tune changed. Now it was coming from the rocks above us. I craned my neck, but I still couldn't see anyone. "Where are you, piper?" I called again. A bark of laughter and another tune, from yet a third location, answered my call. This piper moved fast! I scrambled about, trying to locate him as he played song after song that I'd known in my childhood. Somehow the piper continued to elude me, and my burro was getting mighty confused by all this scrambling about. It was also getting late. If I wanted to make it down into San Miguel County before sunset, I was going to have to leave the saddleback.

Reluctantly I headed down the trail with my burro. The skirling notes of the bagpipes faded away behind me. To my surprise my mood was now one of elation, and I hummed the merry tune of the piper's last song as I walked. My heart was still broken, I knew, but the piper's music had given me hope. There was still beauty here in this wild country—beauty and music. Anything seemed possible after hearing the pipes play.

THE PIPER

I was way down the path when the music broke out one last time. I turned to look back and saw a man in a tattered Highland kilt standing above me, his bagpipes looming over his shoulder. He grinned at me, and I waved. He waved back and then disappeared into the light of the setting sun. I shouted a thank-you to him and headed down toward my new mining camp.

I reached the Minolta mining camp at dusk. As I ate a late supper, I asked the other miners about the piper I'd heard in the hills. An uneasy silence fell over the crowd at my question, and my pulses gave a funny throb at the look I saw on their faces. "Is something wrong?" I asked around a mouthful of beans.

A grizzled miner beside me shook his head gruffly and said, "Some of us have heard him."

"What do you know about him?" I pressed for details.

"Don't ask us about the piper," a red-haired giant of a fellow replied, wiping crumbs from his long beard. "If you want the story, ask the blacksmith over at Sheridan."

I could tell from the looks on the faces around me that I would make no friends here if I continued with that conversation, so I changed the subject, telling the miners all the latest gossip from the Virginius. But I made a mental note to contact the blacksmith at Sheridan at the first possible opportunity.

It wasn't many days later that I made my way to the blacksmith's door to talk to him about a certain piper. The blacksmith, Freddie, went ashen when I broached the subject, and he pulled me inside the smithy where we could speak in private. "Don't you go talking about the piper," he said to me, his huge hands trembling as he laid down his hammer. "That piper is dead. Dead as spent shot. Dead as a coffin nail."

"Dead?" I repeated, shocked. Goose bumps covered my body, and a shudder of sheer ice crawled up my spine. "That's impossible."

"It's true. I dug his body out of the snow with these hands five years ago," Freddie said.

I sank down onto a bench, my head swimming as I took in his words. *That laughing figure, dead?* The thought chilled me, but somehow, it was the fact of his death that caused me pain, not the memory of his ghost.

"Everyone called him Scotty," Freddie said after a moment, taking up his hammer to work on a hot horseshoe. "Nobody could pronounce his real name. He played the pipes for us in the summer, out in the emerald-colored meadows he said reminded him a little of his homeland. He came from Glen Garry in the Grampians, and he was the best of men: hardworking, true hearted, generous, strong as an ox. He worked the Gold Bug claim with the Burn brothers and Jim Walsh. The Gold Bug wasn't too far from the Minolta Mine, so everybody knew him. During the winter he'd play the pennywhistle, since those pipes of his didn't fit into the cabins. Sometimes we'd get all the men together and the fellows would pull out their fiddles and harmonicas and tambourines. Scotty would play the pennywhistle, and we'd sing and dance, clap and holler." Freddie's voice grew wistful as he recalled the impromptu dances of yesteryear.

"What happened?" I asked.

"Avalanche," Freddy said. "The snow ridge above the Gold Bug broke beneath its own weight and swept through the cabin where Scotty and James Burn were bunking down. I heard the rumble and booming thunder of the avalanche from here.

There was nothing we could do in the middle of the night, but we searched the area in the morning and found them buried deep beneath the snow. They were curled up in their beds as if they were still asleep. The avalanche must have crushed Scotty to death instantly."

For a moment there was silence in the forge. Then Freddie spoke up: "We buried Scotty and James down in Telluride. A lot of men died in the avalanches that year." He paused for a moment, his face thoughtful and a little sad. "It gave me quite a turn the first time I heard the pipes in the hills. Now I rather like it."

"I like it too," I said meditatively.

Freddie grinned suddenly. "You're not the only one to see Scotty. He appeared once in the middle of one of our dances, playing the pennywhistle right along with the quartet. Not everyone could see his ghost, but we all heard him!"

I chuckled. "I wonder why I saw him up on the mountain," I said, more to myself than Freddie.

"You're another Highlander," the blacksmith said. "You'd appreciate his music more than all the rest of us put together."

I nodded thoughtfully. It was as good an explanation as any. I thanked Freddie and headed back toward the Minolta, pausing at the base of the trail that led into the mountains to listen for a moment. I heard the faint sound of "Danny Boy" drifting over the mountaintops. I smiled.

"Thanks, Scotty," I called softly up the trail, and then I headed with hope toward the Minolta Mine and my future.

9

Man in the Derby Hat

GOLDEN

I hate riding on trains. Oh, I know, it is much faster than horse and buggy, but at least in a horse and buggy you are out in the fresh air and don't have to deal with ash blowing into your eyes or the smell of coal smoke sticking to your clothing. And the way the train jounces you from side to side in not quite a rhythm so you never get used to it! It makes me sick to my stomach.

When my eldest sent us a telegram early in the summer of 1883 saying she was almost due with her first and would her mama and papa come, I groaned aloud. Not that I wasn't excited about our new grandchild. But our girl had gone West with her new husband a few years ago, and she was living in Golden, the Colorado Territorial capital. That was a mighty long way from our home in New York. The thought of riding in a smelly train among all those strangers and feeling sick for several days did not appeal to me! But Carol was our only daughter, so we agreed to make the trip.

Jerold, my husband, took pity on my nerves and booked our trip in easy stages. We would get off the train and sleep in a hotel each night along the way. Still, by the time we left the station at Denver on the last leg of our trip into Golden, I was heartily sick of the whole business, not to mention heartily sick to my stomach. I told Jerold we were going to buy a house out here, because I wanted nothing more to do with trains ever again! He chuckled and patted my hand, humoring me as if I were kidding!

It was a nice train as far as trains go—rather opulent with fancy seats and brass trimmings. I just wished I felt well enough to enjoy it. The dining car was posh, and the people riding the train were very friendly. The conductors in their crisp uniforms were extremely polite, even when they found me dangling out the window trying not to lose my lunch, or crammed onto the small platform at the end of the train—where riders were not supposed to go—looking green and utterly miserable. They oh so kindly extracted me from these precarious positions and offered me a soothing tonic to help cure my stomach troubles. I only wished the tonics helped.

So sunk in misery was I during the last leg of our journey, I hardly noticed when a cold winter breeze blew suddenly into the car, bringing with it a smell so foul that people around us began gagging. I thought nothing could make my train sickness worse, but that smell hit at the root of my illness, and I flung myself through the open window just in time. I had nothing left to lose, but that didn't stop me from retching miserably out the window. Finally I wiped my mouth with my handkerchief and slid back into my seat beside Jerold.

My patient husband, his nose wrinkled in disgust, was searching irritably for the source of the smell. I knew that he wanted to ream out the person who'd caused his already ill wife so much discomfort. I, meantime, was trying to cope with the sudden cold. My illness already made my skin feel clammy and cold, but now the air inside the car was so chilly we might as well have been sitting on top of one of the snow-capped mountains I saw in the distance, which was strange because it was early summer!

Jerold swore suddenly—something he almost never did—and grabbed my arm so tight it hurt. Irritated, I batted his hand away and followed his gaze down the length of the car, too aware of my roiling stomach to care much about anything else. And then I saw him. A tall man in a black coat and derby hat was coming slowly down the aisle of the train, and the horrible stench was coming directly from his person. But it wasn't the stench that held me transfixed. It was his face under his bushy black beard. His skin was rotting away, the flesh peeling back to reveal white bone in places. And there was a writhing white presence that looked like maggots behind the bones. I arched up, my body stiff with terror. My hands gripped the bottom of the seat so hard my fingers ached. My poor stomach lurched, and I fell sideways against the window, trying to be sick with nothing left to be sick with.

Across the aisle a woman screamed. It echoed up and down the passenger car as people saw the rotting figure walk malevolently among us. I could feel his glare pass over my skin, burning it in the cold manner of frostbite. I also let out a shriek, fumbling for the rosary I kept in my handbag. My scream woke my husband from his daze. He suddenly leapt to his feet and confronted the phantom, shouting: "How dare you frighten my wife!" Then he, too, shrieked as the ghost walked right through his body. Jerold arched up as if in pain.

I found myself on my feet without thought of consequences. "Leave my husband alone!" I roared, flailing my handbag at the

MAN IN THE DERBY HAT

rotting figure. The ghost turned to face me, and bits of his black beard fell off, revealing more rotting skin and bone. He gave me a grimace of sheer hatred. His teeth were so broken they formed razor-sharp edges that cut gashes out of his rotting lips. The look of black malice in his glowing eyes sent me reeling backward as he lifted his arms and bidding dramatically at the lights in the passenger car. At his gesture the lights broke and glass rained down upon me and the other screaming passengers. I flung both arms up to protect my head as shards pierced my clothes and cut my hands and neck. With a chilling laugh, the man in the derby hat vanished, leaving behind chaos and a stench that made the other passengers almost as ill as I was.

The conductor for our car came running when he heard the noise, and he spent the rest of the journey into Golden cleaning up the mess and calming the people in our compartment. Jerold sat white and panting in the seat beside me. The falling glass had cut his face; blood was trickling down his forehead and across one cheek. He was lucky he hadn't lost an eye. But that was nothing to the inner wounds he had suffered when the ghost walked through him. He told me later that it felt as if he'd been pierced in several places by swords made of ice. His insides ached, and he felt violated, as if his mind had been wrenched apart and pawed by the malicious figure.

All in all we made a very poor picture as we stumbled off the train and into the welcoming arms of our daughter and her husband. Carol exclaimed at the sight of my pale green complexion and almost fainted when she saw her father's ravaged face. Jerold muttered an explanation to our son-in-law as they packed us into their wagon and the railroad staff loaded up our trunks.

"A man in a derby hat," our son-in-law exclaimed. "I'd heard rumors of a ghost on the train, but I've never seen him myself. Apparently the man wandered onto the tracks a couple of years back and was run down by a steam train. They never found his body, but his ghost still haunts the line."

"He's an evil, vicious man!" I exclaimed, rearing out of my slumped position to pound the wagon seat with both fists. "He rained glass down on us. You're poor father's face is all cut up! I am never going on that train again as long as I live!" And nothing they said would change my mind.

Poor Jerold had nightmares for weeks following the encounter with the ghost, and it took several days for my constitution to return to normal, so debilitated was I from my train sickness. About the time our first grandchild was born, Jerold wrote to our lawyer back home and put our house on the market, since I had made it abundantly clear that if he wanted to return East, he was going alone. As soon as our house sold, we bought a small ranch outside Golden and settled down to raise horses and spoil our grandchild.

A few days ago, our son wrote to tell us that he and his wife were moving to Golden to be near the rest of us. We were thrilled to get his letter, but I instantly wrote back and advised him to get off the train in Denver when they arrived and hire a carriage for the last leg of the journey to Golden. I didn't want anyone else in my family to fall into the clutches of that demonic phantom in the derby hat.

10

The White Lady

GRAND JUNCTION

My fiancé and I spent a wonderful day hiking Colorado National Monument, and we stopped for a moment to rest on the side of the trail, drinking from our water bottles and discussing the best way to get back to our campsite in Horsethief Canyon. Massive walls of red rock soared magnificently above our heads, and the shadowy place where we sat was already growing cool as evening fell early on the canyon floor.

"Come on, Julie," Harry said, rising and reaching a hand to pull me up. "At this rate, we won't get back until dark!"

I jumped to my feet, and we ambled companionably down the trail leading out of the monument and into the adjacent canyon where we'd pitched our tent. We had decided to celebrate our new engagement with a week of camping and kayaking along the Colorado River, culminating with three days spent hiking in Ruby and Horsethief Canyon and the monument. We were avid outdoors people and were planning a garden wedding in the spring. Meantime, we were enjoying the early fall weather and the lack of competition for campsites along the Colorado. Tourist season was mostly over by now, and we had the place to ourselves. Sweet!

It took an hour to reach the campsite, and by then we were both starving. Harry got a fire going, and soon we had baked beans simmering in the can and potatoes roasting in tinfoil among the coals. After dinner was served, I glanced around our lovely desert surroundings, watching the dusk fall over the world as the first stars twinkled over the mountains.

"So why is this place called Horsethief Canyon?" I asked Harry, stretching my legs lazily toward the fire.

"Two guesses, and the first one doesn't count," my fiancé replied around a mouthful of baked beans.

"Look, I'm not stupid," I said, waving my fork at him. "I figured out that horse thieves must have used this canyon. But surely there's more to the story than that!"

"Just the usual," Harry said dismissively. "Horse thieves hid out here with their stolen horses, and one day the sheriff got wise and tracked them down. There was a gunfight, men and horses got killed, and the sheriff's posse took prisoners and returned the horses to their rightful owners. End of story."

Harry is a sweet man and I love him dearly, but he does not possess a romantic bone in his entire body.

"Honestly, Harry," I said, setting aside my plate. "I could have told a better story than that."

Harry snorted inelegantly. "Yeah, I can just hear your version!" He raised his voice to a soprano squeak and dictated: "It was a tale of passion and romance set against the rugged desert sky. A man, his one true love, and the horse that stood between them!" He waved his hands dramatically.

I got the giggles and rolled a bit on the red rock that was my seat by the fire. "You sound like one of those old films they made in the forties," I choked.

"No, *you* sound like a film from the forties," Harry said teasingly. "I was just imitating the way you sound when you tell stor—" His voice broke off suddenly, and his cheeks went ashen in the firelight. He was staring over my shoulder, and a shudder passed through me. Whatever could have made my brave, practical fiancé look like that? A rattlesnake? A cougar? I froze, and then very cautiously peered over my shoulder.

Darkness had settled over the canyon as we ate dinner. Normally I would not have been able to see anything outside our circle of fire except the twinkling stars far above us. But now a white light illuminated the red canyon walls around us. The light emanated from a woman wearing a long dress that might have been in style in the 1880s but was severely out-of-date now. The white lady was walking restlessly across the canyon, heading toward the cliff on the far side. Her glowing boots were several inches above the ground.

My mouth fell open in shock, and shivers of fear ran up my arms and legs. I could scarcely credit what I was seeing. It was a ghost! It could be nothing else. The look on the woman's face mixed fear with determination. She glanced from side to side, as if searching for someone. Her hair was tied up under a poke bonnet, but there were loose tendrils on either side of her worried face; they blew backward as if she was caught in a windstorm, while her skirts flapped about as if caught in a gale. But there was no wind stirring on that warm September evening.

"Harry," I gasped, inching backward toward my fiancé. The glowing figure seriously spooked me. It was so uncanny, so not of this world. I felt Harry grip my arms reassuringly, though his hands were cold and shaking against my bare skin. We watched speechlessly as the white lady crossed the canyon. She kept walking when she reached the cliff, and she disappeared into the red rock wall. Instantly the canyon plunged into darkness, save for the flickering fire behind us.

"Oh! Oh!" I gave a shriek more of shock than fear and whirled to press my face against Harry's shoulder. He hugged me so tight it hurt, and I knew without a word passing between us that he was as shaken by the sight of the ghost as I was. Suddenly he gave a gasp of surprise and called: "There she is again!"

I turned around in his arms and looked where he pointed. The white lady had emerged from the end of the canyon and was walking along the banks of the Colorado River, still searching restlessly for someone or something. The river glowed in the alien white light that surrounded her, and I could see the ripples of the current as it flowed past the specter on its bank. The white lady looked up suddenly, glancing over at our campfire as if she truly saw us. Her face was crumpled with frustration and growing fear, as if the hope that had driven her to pace along this canyon was fading into despair. She suddenly covered her face with her hands and vanished with a small popping sound that echoed loudly among the cliffs.

My whole body was shaking, and goose bumps were crawling along my arms and legs. "I want to go home right now," I said shrilly, clutching Harry's arm.

"We can't kayak out of here at night, Julie," Harry said, his voice sounding far too calm for him to really be calm, if you get what I mean.

"I am not staying here with a ghost," I said, my voice rising on the last word until it was almost a shriek. I felt ashamed of

THE WHITE LADY

myself, but my body was shaking so badly I could hardly stand. Harry was holding me upright, or I would have fallen.

"Why don't you get in the tent, Jewels," Harry said, using the pet name he'd given me when we first started dating. "The ghost won't bother you in the tent."

And how would he know that? I thought hysterically. But he was right; we couldn't kayak out of here at night. At least the tent *seemed* like a refuge.

Harry helped me over to it, and I crawled inside. I heard him dousing the fire and cleaning up from dinner. A few minutes later he crawled in beside me and pulled me into his arms, sleeping bag and all. I huddled close to him, still shivering.

"Where's your sense of romance, Jewels?" he whispered against my hair. "This would make a perfect 1940s film. A man on the run steals the heart of a lovely maiden. She tries to shield him from the law, but he is tracked down and killed in a shootout in Horsethief Canyon. She dies of a broken heart, and ever after her ghost roams the canyon in search of her one true love."

"Do you really think the ghost is related to the shootout in the canyon?" I asked Harry. His story had calmed me somewhat, and my breathing was almost back to normal.

"I have no idea," Harry said into my ear. "But it makes a good story."

It did make a good story, and it reconciled me to the ghost's presence—at least enough to allow me to fall asleep. But I was up at dawn the next morning, and we were out of that haunted canyon as fast as we could pack our things and load the kayaks. One ghost sighting was enough for me!

11

Maggie

CRIPPLE CREEK

When he took the job at the Colorado Grande Casino, the new security guard did not believe in ghosts. The casino was set up in the three-story Fairley Brothers & Lampman Block Building in Cripple Creek, home of the famous Independence lode, one of the largest gold strikes in history. The landmark building on the corner of Bennett Avenue and Third Street once housed a mortuary, a drugstore, a barbershop, office space for prominent physicians and attorneys, and the Elks Club. Now a restaurant occupied the old mortuary, and a casino dominated the rest of the building.

The security guard liked working in Cripple Creek. The historic boom-turned-ghost town was a magnet for tourists, and the folks working on famous Bennett Street were friendly and welcoming. Maggie's Restaurant in the basement of his workplace had good food at good prices, though he was sometimes bothered by the smell of an old-fashioned floral perfume that wafted through the room. It wasn't until after he'd eaten there a few times that he learned the restaurant was named for the ghost that supposedly haunted the building. It was Maggie's perfume that he smelled when he ate in the restaurant, according to stories told by the staff. They also reported that Maggie's high-heeled shoes were often heard walking in the second and third stories of the building, and sometimes, a woman's laughter drifted down the stairs. People speculated that Maggie was connected with one of the doctors who had rented office space in the building, but no one really knew who she was in life.

The security guard shrugged off the stories. He'd always lumped ghost stories in with fairy tales; something to tell the kiddies, but he'd never seen a ghost, and seeing was believing.

One evening, while working the graveyard shift, the security guard was sipping coffee and gazing at the video monitor when a light sprang on in the darkened game room he was viewing. A young woman appeared on the screen, sitting in front of a lit slot machine. He gasped and jumped to his feet in surprise, spilling his coffee. He hardly noticed the sting of hot liquid against his skin, as he was so intent on the picture in front of him. The woman wore a fancy dress with a skirt that flared down to the floor, a silk shirtwaist, and a lacy concoction at her neck. Her dark hair was piled high under tortoiseshell combs, and her eyes danced as she worked the slot machine.

A tall gentleman then joined her. He was wearing a long black coat that reached the knees of his formal striped trousers and a fancy top hat that made him look nearly a foot taller than his actual height. One of his hands rested caressingly on the shoulder of the pretty woman, and the other pointed toward the flashing lights of the slot machine. He was laughing, and she glanced coquettishly up at him, her dark eyes shining with happiness.

"How in blazes did they get in there?" the security guard wondered, grabbing his flashlight. The casino was locked up

MAGGIE

tight as a drum. Surely he would have seen them entering the building on one of the cameras?

He raced through the dark building toward the gaming room, realizing he might lose his job over this incident. Two people had illegally entered the building on his watch! And now they were playing the slots, bold as brass.

He reached the top of the stairs within a minute or two of spying the couple on the video camera and stopped in shock. The gaming room was dark and silent. No lights flashed, no woman sat at the slot machine with her top-hatted escort beside her. The room was empty.

It couldn't be! It was impossible. Surely they'd heard him coming and were hiding somewhere. He ran down the stairs, flashing his light behind every machine, searching in every dark corner for the intruders. He found nothing. Angry, frustrated, and confused, the security guard returned to the office. He glanced in the camera array and found the gaming room dark in the video monitor. He shook his head, trying to clear his thoughts. Had he dozed off somehow and dreamed the whole thing? He didn't feel sleepy.

He reached over and rewound the tape, torn between wishing for validation of the incident and hoping that it had never happened at all. A moment later he was staring at the image of a woman in fancy Victorian dress sitting in front of the slot machine, her laughing escort beside her, gesturing toward the flashing lights. Suddenly they vanished from the screen, and he saw a picture of himself peering down the staircase into the empty gaming room. The security guard watched himself search the room, growing more angry and frustrated with each passing moment. He gazed intently at the video monitor as his image stomped out of the gaming room, complete bafflement on his face. As he disappeared from view, the lights came on again in the gaming room, and the man and woman were once again playing the slot machine and laughing. He watched them in stunned silence as they played another round or two and then vanished as instantly as they had appeared.

They were ghosts! They had to be. There was no other explanation for what he was viewing. He broke out in a cold sweat, his hands trembling as he stopped the tape and pulled it from the service, placing it rather too hastily upon a shelf. He'd review the tape again after he finished his shift. At the moment, he still had a job to do.

When his supervisor arrived the next morning, the security guard discussed the incident with him. The supervisor wanted to review the tape with him, so the security guard reached up to the shelf where he'd placed the the incriminating video the night before. The tape had vanished! The two men looked at one another, nonplussed, and the security guard felt goose bumps crawling over his skin.

As he hurried home after his shift, the security guard pondered the advisability of working in a haunted building. Remembering the incandescent face of the young woman at the slot machine, he found it impossible to remain afraid. If that was Maggie, she meant him no harm. She only wanted a little fun. And who was her handsome escort? Her husband? A boyfriend? He'd probably never know. He just hoped he'd have as much fun when he was a ghost himself! Smiling, he let himself into his house, ready for a snack and some shut-eye.

12

Vindicator

SAND CREEK MASSACRE NATIONAL HISTORIC SITE

I passed a man sitting cross-legged on the ground as I made my way toward the monument at Sand Creek Massacre National Historic Site. He was wearing the traditional garb of the Cheyenne people, and he was chanting softly to himself. I tiptoed past, not wanting to disturb his meditations at this sacred spot where so many had perished.

I clutched the National Park Service pamphlet, crumpling it slightly in my sweaty hands. It was a hot day on the prairie, and a haze made the distant horizon shimmer. But I felt cold inside, terribly cold. I did not want to be here. The story of the Sand Creek Massacre made me writhe inside my skin whenever I thought of what the Third Colorado Regiment had done here. But I felt strongly that I needed to visit, to honor the dead. And so I had driven down from the mountains, leaving my husband and children to their own devices while I made this pilgrimage.

According to my reading, it was the influx of gold miners into Colorado Territory that had caused tensions between the Native Americans and the settlers to escalate into armed conflict. John Chivington, the Fighting Preacher, was looking to win a political nomination by making himself a hero, so he played upon the settlers' fears, railing against the governor's easy stance concerning the Cheyenne and Arapaho until a regiment was raised to deal with the supposed trouble. When he set out with the Third Colorado, Chivington was determined to fight any Indians he could find, thus winning himself fame and the political career he craved.

When no Cheyenne dog soldiers could be found, the Fighting Preacher set out to conquer a peaceful native encampment on the Big Bend of Sand Creek filled with women, children, and the elderly. The village was under the leadership of Chief Black Kettle, a pacifist; therefore, it had only a few warriors to protect the people living within. They had come to this place seeking to avoid conflict. But on the morning of November 29, 1864, troops from the Third Colorado, led by Chivington, came thundering down on the encampment, ignoring the white flag of truce and the American flag that were quickly hoisted above Chief Black Kettle's lodge.

I stared unseeing at the simple low monument before me, at the sandy creek and the low scrub. The chill inside me grew worse as I recalled the history of this place. I set off blindly along the bed of the creek, hating what had been done here and hating myself for being a descendant of one of the men who had fought in the Third Colorado that day.

As I walked, I felt as if I were caught in a bubble of time, halfway between the past and the present. The scene around me remained the same, but I could hear soft voices chanting in the prairie wind, rising and falling as if in prayer. Out of the corner of my eye, I glimpsed an encampment full of tepees, but when I turned my head, I saw nothing but prairie beyond the bend in the creek. I heard a dog bark, a child yell in delight, a woman call anxiously. I saw nothing.

I don't remember how long I ambled about in this suspended state before I realized I was no longer walking alone. The Cheyenne man I'd seen when I entered the historic site was beside me. I hadn't heard him approach. He was just there. Still in a daze, I accepted his presence easily, as if I had been expecting him.

"You are troubled," he said as we walked through the prairie grass.

"This place disturbs me," I said miserably. "My people did terrible things here."

He nodded in sober agreement. "It is true. The things done in this place were terrible indeed. But *you* did not do them."

"I am descended from one who did," I said bitterly. "I've read some of his letters. He was proud of what he'd done. He spoke of scalping children and killing women who were on their knees, begging for mercy. He called himself a *vindicator*." I spat out the last word as if it were a curse.

We walked silently for a time. Then, in a dry unemotional voice, he described for me the chaos of that terrible day in November. The sound of musket fire and artillery shattering the quiet peace of the village. The thunder of nearly seven hundred horsemen bearing down upon the village as the cavalry charged. Warriors scrambling for horses and weapons. Women and children screaming in panic, fleeing every which way. Teenagers and old men staying behind to face the companies crossing Sand Creek, defending the haphazard retreat. Blood flowing everywhere. Frightened Cheyenne and Arapaho digging themselves into defendable pits along the creek.

VINDICATOR

"The men ripped women apart with their knives. They clubbed little children to death, until their brains spilled out upon the ground," the elderly man said, his dark eyes fixed on the far horizon. "We were scalped, beaten, mutilated, torn apart. The fetters of civilization were set aside by the soldiers who attacked us that day. It was the white men who acted like savages. We just ran. And died."

Tears poured down my face as he spoke. I was too choked up to reply, even if I'd had anything to say. The elderly man stopped suddenly and handed me a soft white handkerchief, seemingly conjured from nowhere. I wiped my eyes and blew my nose, then gazed from the soiled handkerchief to the elderly Cheyenne in apology.

"I'll have it cleaned," I said quickly.

"Keep it," he said with a little smile. Then he sobered and said: "I have a message for you, Cheryl."

I jumped, wondering how he knew my name.

"People like you make a difference. You are the opposite of your forefather. You are a vindicator for all that is right and true and just." His dark eyes bored deeply into my blue ones. "Do not forget this. And do not forget me."

I blinked back a second onrush of tears and lifted my chin. His words warmed my chilled heart. I knew I would remember them. And I sensed that in the years to come, I would be forever changed because he had spoken them.

"I will not forget your words," I said. "But I do not know your name."

He smiled, and it transformed his face.

"My name is Black Kettle," he said. And then he vanished.

I blinked in astonishment, and the sights and smells of the present day came crashing down around me in a rush of light and color and sound. I found myself standing before the Sand Creek Massacre Monument in the exact place I had been when I first arrived. It was as if my walk along the creek bed had never happened. I shook my head, trying to clear it. Had the last half hour been a waking dream? Was I losing my mind?

A warm wind blew softly against my hair, and the scent of dust and prairie grass filled my nostrils, making me sneeze. I reached up to blot my nose, and then I paused in shock. In my right hand I still clutched a white handkerchief.

PART TWO

Powers of Darkness and Light

13

The Telegram

PALMER LAKE

I was working as the night chief at a telegraph office in Denver when the mysterious call came through from an in-state office identifying itself as AZ. Now, I know all the Colorado telegraph office codes; it was one of the first things I learned when I took this job. AZ isn't one of them.

"Someone is messing around," I told the man operating the telegraph. "Let's see what happens if I take the key." He nodded, grinning slyly, knowing I did not suffer fools gladly.

"Here you go, Chief," he said, rising and bowing me into his station. I stepped to the telegraph key, identified myself, and asked the AZ office to identify itself. The remote operator just wired that he was a small relaying office that had an urgent collect message from "K.S." (Kansas City—the phantom telegrapher signed the original telegram "K.S."). I frowned for a moment in thought and then had them send the message through. It came so fast my fingers were numb trying to keep up with it. It read as follows:

> *I grave was my a in man easy who rest in not my*
> *will time I on deciphered earth, is drank message*

considerable this and Until one .divide night or
was ridgeway killed continental on the what as is
known known is as what the on continental killed
ridgeway was or night divide. one Until and this
considerable, message drank is earth deciphered
on I time will my not in rest who easy man in a
my was grave. I
    Llaksah dr

I stared at the telegram, nonplussed. It was unsigned, and I didn't recognize the name of the person to whom it was being sent.

The operator looked over my shoulder. "Looks like some kind of code," he said, "but I'm darned if I know the key to it." He glanced sideways at me to see if I'd reprimand him for the *darned.* I had strict rules about swearing in my office, but darned was on my acceptable list.

"Send the message on," I said. "See if they can find this A. Towser, 26 Flower Lane, to whom it's been addressed. Maybe he knows where the AZ relaying office is."

"Yes, Chief," the operator said and carried it away with him. I sent a quick wire to Kansas City inquiring about the message and then turned away when another operator hailed me from the far side of the office. Back to work. I put the mystery message out of my mind.

The next night, there were three messages waiting for me when I stepped into my office. One was the mysterious message with a note attached to it that said A. Towser was unknown in Denver and Flower Lane didn't exist. The second was from Kansas City, saying the mystery message had not originated from its office. And the third was a second telegram from the mysterious AZ relaying office. It was an exact duplicate of the first, save that it was addressed to another unknown individual. "Curiouser and curiouser," I muttered to myself, quoting *Alice in Wonderland,* the current favorite novel of my young daughter.

I went out onto the main floor to ask about the second telegram. The young fellow who'd taken the message said the operator who had sent it from the nonexistent AZ office had signed himself KX.

"Never heard of him," I said, fascinated. I didn't approve of folks breaking the rules or sending expensive telegrams collect, but I loved puzzles, and this one was a dilly!

"Nearly broke my fingers trying to keep up with KX," the young man confessed. "Whoever he is, he's fast!" Remembering my own difficulties from the night before, I nodded in agreement.

I sent messages to all the in-state offices to be on the lookout for telegrams from either the AZ relaying office or an operator called KX. Then I went back to my office to get on with the paperwork.

Over the next several weeks, KX sent us his mysterious message every night. The telegrams were said to have originated from many different cities, though Denver was never one of them, and they always came through the AZ relaying office. I carefully read the mysterious message repeatedly, trying to make heads or tails of it. Nothing. I needed the key to the code.

If I was in the office when KX sent his message, I would telegraph back immediately, telling him we couldn't read his message. "Take it to the cable clerks," KX telegraphed back. We did, but they had no better luck than I did.

I was curious. I was upset. I wanted to find KX and give him a piece of my mind for disrupting my orderly night office. Instead I telegraphed the nonexistent AZ relaying office and said: "Darn it, give me a key!" I wasn't expecting an answer, but one came through a minute later. "1,3. 1,3. Forward, backward. Either way okay."

My eyes widened. So simple! I grabbed a copy of the telegram from my desk and started reading every other word. And KX was correct. The message read the same forward and backward. It said:

> *I was a man who in my time on Earth drank*
> *considerable, and one night was killed on what*
> *is known as the continental ridgeway or divide.*
> *Until this message is deciphered, I will not rest*
> *easy in my grave.*
>   *—R. D. Haskall*

A chill ran through my body, and goose bumps pricked up all over my arms and legs. The telegram was from a ghost! We had a specter on the wire. I broke out into a cold sweat, and my hands trembled so bad they made the paper rattle. Everyone in the office was staring at me.

"Did you solve it, chief?" one of the operators asked in a diffident tone. I nodded and read the message aloud to my staff. We'd be trying to solve the puzzle for weeks now. They deserved to know. A few folks gasped when they realized what the telegram meant. One fellow turned white as a sheet and had to be helped into a chair.

"So what now?" asked the night operator who took the very first message from KX.

"Now we ask," I said grimly. I opened my key, contacted the AZ relaying office, and typed in "Don't 13," which is telegraph speak for "I don't understand." The whole staff clustered around me, waiting breathlessly for a response. A moment later the sounder rattled to life, conveying a new message in flawless Morse. When deciphered using the same key as the first, it said:

> *I was a telegrapher who at one time worked*
> *in New York State. In 1849 I caught the gold*
> *fever and came West. I drank considerably and*
> *was killed one night in a drunken brawl out on*
> *the old Pueblo trail, fifteen miles from what is*
> *now Palmer Lake on the Continental Divide.*
> *I cannot rest in my grave. My spirit is tied to*
> *Earth until I make known the cause of my death.*
> *The telegraph pole from which I am sending*
> *this is planted directly over my grave, the butt*
> *of the pole resting on my breast. I will call you*
> *up regularly for three nights, and if I raise you,*
> *answer. My message reads backward the same as*
> *forward.*
> *—R. D. Haskall*

There was a long silence when I finished reading the new message. On the desk the circuit remained opened, as if it were listening for our response. Suddenly two of my operators laughed. "It's a joke. It has to be," one of them exclaimed. The sounder clattered suddenly: "no joke." Then the circuit was cut off from the other end.

"Permission to find the pole, chief?" one of the two disbelievers asked. "We can catch the joker red-handed the next time he keys in."

I nodded. The two operators grinned triumphantly and turned away to plan their journey. I glanced at the others still clustered around my desk. Their faces were pale, and I saw that I was not the only one who thought the spirit's message was real. I gave another nod of understanding, and a sigh went up from everyone still present.

"I wouldn't go to that pole if you paid me a king's ransom in gold," muttered one youngster as the operators returned to their posts. I saw more than one head nod in agreement.

The two skeptics were gone for two nights. On the first night, a message came from KX saying: "Do you believe me? Answer please." I telegraphed back. "I believe. Not all here do. I am sending two skeptics to your pole." On the second night, a longer message came through, and I smiled when I read it and sent off a quick acknowledgment. Then I sat down to wait. My skeptics would return to their duties the following night.

On the third evening, two ashen-faced operators came sheepishly into my office. "We followed the road out from Palmer Lake, heading toward the divide," the more senior operator said when I asked for his report. "We counted each pole until we reach the fifteen-mile mark. There we stopped and settled down to wait for our joker. We waited all afternoon and into the evening. It had just grown dark when we saw . . . we

THE TELEGRAM

saw—" he broke off in distress and glanced appealingly at his younger companion.

The junior operator squared his shoulders, took a deep breath, and said: "The air got real cold around us, worse than anything I've felt in winter. Then we saw a light appear at the bottom of the pole. A glowing vapor poured out of the ground all around the pole, and it became the figure of a man. He was th . . . throbbing from white light to blue. It made my eyes water. And he held a telegraph key in his glowing hand!"

The junior operator paused, his body trembling at the memory. A shudder went through my body, and I goose bumps covered my body as I listened to the tale. I nodded to the senior operator to finish the story.

The older man had to clear his throat twice before he continued. "The . . . the specter climbed to the top of the pole and cut into the wires. Then he telegraphed something on his key. When he was done, he slid down the pole and kept right on going when he reached the ground, sort of flowing into it like water goes down a drain, until there was nothing left but the darkness."

Both men gulped then, and I saw that they were sweating in the strain of their storytelling. Without saying a word, I handed them the translation of the telegram the ghost had sent last night:

> *Your two investigators here. They have seen me.*
> *Farewell to Earth. I have been heard and seen. I*
> *am satisfied. Good-bye.*
>   *—R. D. Haskall*

The two men stared from the message to me and back, speechless. "Well done," I said after a moment. I waved them out of my office to tell the rest of the staff what they'd seen.

I closed my door when they were gone, and for the last time I opened a circuit to the AZ relaying station. "My skeptics have reported in as true believers. Well done," I typed. The sounder rattled back immediately: "Thank .you you. Thank." With a sad smile, I typed back: "Rest in peace, my friend." I received an acknowledgment of receipt, but no reply. None was needed.

We never heard from R. D. Haskall again.

14

Unexpected Witness

EUREKA

I frowned down at the page of notes in my hand. The lantern flickered in a light breeze that came through my office window as I glared at the paper, willing the words to change. But alas, no amount of willing could alter this case. I had been an attorney for many years and had developed a sixth sense that told me when my clients were guilty and when they were innocent. My sixth sense had never been wrong, and it was telling me my client—Christopher Johnson—was innocent. However, my intuition was not admissible as evidence in court, and the evidence that was admissible, though circumstantial, was incriminating in the extreme.

Johnson had motive—oh, boy, did he have motive. The murdered man had won a lawsuit against him over some mining property. Johnson had been seen in the vicinity of the victim's cabin on the night Jack Wilson was murdered. Johnson was known to own a large hunter's dirk, and the victim had been murdered with a very large knife that had perforated his chest multiple times and had almost severed both his arms and his head.

Actually, I was surprised that Johnson was still alive. Wilson was very popular among his fellow miners, and it was only

Johnson's prompt arrest that kept him from being lynched by a mob. At the moment, a double guard protected Johnson at the prison to discourage anyone from breaking in and hanging the man before he got to trial.

I got some ugly stares from the townsmen lounging near the jail when I went to visit the suspect earlier this evening. A few of them jeered at me for taking the case, and I was forced to remind them that a person was supposed to be innocent until proven guilty.

"He's already been proven guilty," snapped one of Wilson's friends.

"Not by a judge and jury he hasn't," I replied with dignity. I stared at the man until he flushed and turned away.

When I entered his cell, Johnson looked up at me without hope. I sat awkwardly on the bed opposite him and asked him to repeat his story once again. He claimed to have been walking to the mine, where he had been asked to take the night shift for a friend. He had just passed Wilson's cabin, he recalled, which was directly on the trail to the mine, when he was taken ill with a stomach malady. He said he returned home to sleep off his sickness without reporting in to the mine. No one had seen him leave or return to his cabin, although a few of the men on the night shift had seen him on the path leading to the mine. Worse, Johnson claimed that his knife had disappeared from his cabin on the day before the murder. I stared into the man's eyes as he spoke, and I knew in my gut he wasn't lying. But there was no proof of his innocence, and even he did not believe he would be set free.

Now back in my office I threw my pen down on top of my notes in my frustration, spattering ink everywhere. I was too tired to think straight, so I laid down on the couch in my office to get some rest, still wondering how I could convince a jury that my client was innocent. It was a puzzle I could not solve. Finally, I blew out the lantern and fell into a restless sleep.

I awoke suddenly, my body frozen into stillness, aware that I was no longer alone in the room. I peered carefully through my eyelashes, remembering that I had left my pistol in the desk drawer where it would not be easy to reach. To my surprise the room was filled with an eerie flickering blue light. Silhouetted against the unnatural light was the figure of a woman in a heavy veil. She moved toward my prone figure and intoned in a voice that sounded faint and far away: "Christie Johnson is innocent of the crime of which he is charged."

My heart slammed in my throat, and I was filled with a sudden excitement. I didn't know who this woman was, and at the moment I didn't care. She could play all the funny light tricks she wanted, as long as she gave me something to help clear my client. "How can I prove it?" I asked eagerly.

"I will be at the trial and will give my testimony," said the faint voice from the veiled silhouette. As I opened my mouth to question her further, the veiled figure vanished. And the blue light went out.

I gasped in astonishment, and my body went all cold and shaky for a moment. It took three tries for me to get the lantern lit, and then I examined every window, every door. They were all locked. Finally I sank down onto the couch with my head in my hands. Had I dreamed the whole thing? I didn't know how to answer that question, any more than I knew how to clear my client of the charges against him. I lay down again on the couch, but I didn't fall asleep again that night.

I entered the courtroom two days later, still at a loss. The best appeal I could make would probably not be good enough to clear Johnson, and I had no idea if the veiled woman had been a bad dream or just a figment of my imagination. Or—the thought crossed my mind—she might have been what my grandmother called a forerunner. A forerunner was a vision or a premonition of what is to come. Granny had stories of lights appearing outside of a house where someone was doomed to die and tales of people who had spirit traveled in their dreams to speak to loved ones or to warn someone of approaching ill fate. The veiled woman had said she would testify today in court, so obviously she had to be alive to do so. Had she been spirit walking in her dreams when she appeared to me? I shook my head to clear it. It was probably nonsense. I had dreamed up the whole thing. I squared my shoulders and went to take my place at the defendant's table.

The room was crowded with sensation seekers from surrounding mining camps. Word of the horrible crime had spread quickly, and the men filling the room had already condemned my client in their minds. Johnson was brought in under heavy guard, and angry looks were cast upon him from every side. *Was it possible for the jury to be impartial under such circumstances?* I wondered with a sinking heart.

When my client pleaded not guilty to the murder charge, the room erupted in hisses and shouts, and the crier had to roar repeatedly to restore order. The district attorney opened the case with a rousing speech about the bloodthirsty nature of the crime and then called witness after witness to testify against my client.

Then it was my turn. I gave perhaps the very best speech of my career, warning the jury that the blood of a guiltless man would be on their heads if they condemned my client on purely circumstantial evidence. I had no witnesses to call and was about to close for the defense when a paper was thrust into my hands. It said: "Call Mary Powers." My heart leapt into my throat. Could it be? Turning to the court, I said: "May it please your honor, I have one witness to examine." I handed the paper to the crier, who called Mary Powers to the stand. A small commotion ensued from the back of the room, and then a heavily veiled woman dressed in all black stepped forward. I immediately recognized my midnight visitor. When she arrived at the stand, she threw back her veil, revealing the most classically beautiful face I have ever beheld. Her loveliness took my breath for a moment, until I saw the lines of care around her eyes and mouth. I was not alone in my wonder. A stir passed through the crowd, and every eye in the jury was fixed upon her as she was sworn in. At my rather incoherent prompting, she told us the following story:

I was born and raised in the East, and there I met a handsome young man who was introduced to my family through letters of recommendation given to him by a mutual friend. His frequent visits to our house resulted in an engagement between us, but he put off naming the day of marriage, although—to my shame—he did not put off other matters that should be saved for marriage. After causing my ruin, he fled the East Coast rather than put matters to right, and I fell ill for many weeks, hovering between life and death in a terrible fever that would not break.

For a moment her voice faltered. She bowed her head and took a couple of deep breaths. Then she looked up, tears bright upon her cheeks, and continued:

> *Recovery came to me at last, and with it a terrible thirst for revenge against the man who had betrayed me. For years I sought news of this man, and my weary waiting was rewarded at last when I learned he had come to Colorado to look for gold. I followed at once, and made cautious inquiries about him when I reached the territory. Those inquiries led me at last to a remote cabin. As I approached along the path, fate took a hand, for my eyes beheld a glint of sunlight coming from a knife that had been dropped upon the ground. This knife . . .*

She pulled out a large hunting dirk that belonged to Johnson. She held it high for all to see and then continued her tale. "I peered in the window of the cabin and saw my betrayer—the man calling himself Jack Wilson—asleep on his bed. I crept into the cabin and over to his bed, and plunged the knife into his heart. And then," she hesitated, swallowed, and looked down at the knife in her hands. "I think the sight of his blood maddened me, for suddenly I was screaming a list of his crimes at the top of my lungs as I stabbed blindly at my betrayer again and again. I don't remember leaving the cabin, or much of anything else since then."

The woman calling herself Mary Powers gazed suddenly at my client, and her beautiful lips quivered as their eyes met.

UNEXPECTED WITNESS

There was a look on her face that I couldn't read, though I sensed it was important.

Mary Powers tore her gaze away from Johnson at last and looked over at the jury. Her face twisted until a manic caricature of hate devoured its loveliness, and she cried: "The only thing that matters now is that I have had my revenge!" And so saying, she plunged the knife into her own breast and slumped over, hot blood pouring all over the floor.

The courtroom erupted with shrill cries of horror and confusion. It was not until the woman's dead body was carried out that order was at last restored. Upon instruction from the judge, the jury rendered a unanimous verdict of not guilty for my client without even leaving their seats to deliberate. Johnson was in a daze as we left the courthouse together. He could not believe he had been set free by the testimony of that lovely, demented woman.

"Why?" Johnson asked me in bewilderment. "Why did she do it? She didn't know me. I was just some dumb miner who could have taken the fall for her. Anyone else would have made a clean getaway and left me to hang! Why did she turn herself in?"

I had no answer for him. I'd caught a glimpse of something in Mary Powers's face when she looked at my client, but I had been unable to interpret her expression. And now I would never know.

The woman was buried in a grove of pine trees near the trail to the mine. There was no name to put on her tomb, save that of Mary Powers, which was probably an alias. There was no one to inform of her death, for she had left nothing to identify herself behind. Hers was a lonely grave, though not one unadorned, for there were always wildflowers placed beside the simple cross. Once I saw Johnson sneaking into the grove of pines, a posy of flowers in his big hands and a look of half-defiant shame on his ruggedly handsome features. And it was in that moment that I finally understood why Mary Powers had turned herself in. She'd fallen in love with my client—and had died to make things right.

15

Haunted Spring

I had a hankering to do some prospecting out along the gulch that spring, so I hired me a half-native guide to show me the most promising places. He had a Spanish papa who'd bequeathed him the name of Martinez, but he was raised by his Ute mama, and he knew the backcountry better than anyone. So when he proposed going to a promising site up near the Pau-to-creeda spring, I was all ears.

Martinez waxed eloquent over the proposed new diggings, and I asked him why in tarnation he hadn't mentioned it before. We'd been hacking around the mountains for more than two weeks with not a nugget to our names.

"It was not an auspicious time to go near the Pau-to-creeda," he told me in all seriousness. "The spirit of the creek, she is vindictive. One goes there only with great care, and only when the time is right."

"And is the time right now?" I asked sarcastically. Martinez nodded fervently, ignoring my tone. And off he went, over ridge, through canyon, and up and over some of the biggest dad-blame mountains you'd ever want to climb. We ran out of water in our canteens before we ran out of mountain, and unfortunately for us, this particular path was a dry one. I kept trying to veer off the trail to search for water in the lower reaches, but Martinez claimed he couldn't find the place we were seeking unless he stuck to the high places. So we labored on.

It was sunset when Martinez gave an exclamation of satisfaction. "There," he said, pointing to a gulch across the way. It was a picturesque spot with gnarled pine trees and towering buttresses of granite. But all I could think about was water, and when I saw a fountain of water springing forth from an overhang down in the gulch, I gave a shout of joy and aimed myself in that direction without further ado. The rest of the gulch was devoid of vegetation, but the area just below the spring was a lovely green mound of grass, with vines clambered cheerfully over the rocks all around the watering hole.

"No, no! Stop!" Martinez cried, pulling me back onto the path.

"What do you mean stop?" I shouted, turning to face him with a snarl. "We ain't got water, and we need some, pronto."

"That is the cursed spring!" Martinez said. "Pau-to-creeda. It is said that those who drink of it drink only once—never again!"

"There ain't no curse gonna keep me from that water," I said grimly. "You lead the way down, or I'll make you do the Texas two-step." I purposefully patted the pistol at my side.

"Be it on your own head," Martinez muttered and led me on a circuitous path down into the gulch toward the "haunted" spring. It was twilight by the time we reached it. Little birds were hopping and chirruping cheerfully as I raced the last few steps and flung myself down to take a drink of the cold, cold water. Martinez pulled me up before I could get a sip, saying, "I beg you, do not drink. You will regret this!"

I slapped his hand away. "The birds don't mind your spirit. Why should I?"

"It is not safe to drink here. There is another spring farther down in the gulch where the water is safe."

"Forget it!" I said roughly and drank my fill right then and there. It was the best water I'd ever tasted, pure and sweet. "Well," I said at last, sitting back on my heels. "This seems like a good place to make camp."

Martinez went pale. "Not here. We have already stayed too long."

"Listen, mister," I said, patting my pistol again. "I hired you to scout me out some gold. So I'm the boss, remember? And I say we stay here tonight."

Martinez gave in with bad grace. He was silent and sullen as he made a fire and prepared our dinner. He kept as far away from the haunted spring as he could, as if he feared the spirit would lunge out and grab him if he got too close. By this time I was curious to know what it was about the Pau-to-creeda spring that made him so jumpy. I asked him about it, and he told me the following story.

Long ago, the Utes and Navajos were at war with one another. The Utes had been driven far to the north of the Gila River, once the boundary between the two lands. However, a great chief name Cotero came to power among the Utes, and he won back much of the land the tribe had lost to its enemy. About this time, the old chief of the Navajos perished. The new chief, Tahindra, was more inclined to spend time enjoying his new power and his new wife, rather than seek warfare and expansion.

Given the change in leadership, Cotero decided it was time to seek peace with the enemy tribe. But when he and his advisers arrived at the council of tribes and wise men, the Navajo chief was not. Cotero refused to enter into a treaty if Tahindra was not present at the council, and so the new Navajo chief reluctantly left his home and came to the council, bringing his new wife and family with him.

The moment Cotero saw Tahindra's lovely young wife he wanted the woman for himself, no matter what the cost. And so he arranged for her to be kidnapped and brought to a secret hiding place a day's journey away. But the Ute braves captured the beautiful young sister-in-law of the Navajo chief, mistaking her for his wife, and the maiden herself perpetuated the deception in order to save her sister.

Tahindra was enraged when he learned of the abduction and ordered all the Utes remaining at the intertribal council site put to death. As for Cotero, he tried to salvage the situation by proposing to the beautiful young maiden in place of her sister. But she scorned his offer, and so he imprisoned her in the gulch by the spring and sent word to the Navajos that she would be held in secret until peace was agreed upon and a large portion of the Navajo territory given to Cotero as ransom.

Urged on by his wife, the Navajo chief waged war upon Cotero, but the Ute chief was a fierce warrior. In the ensuing battle the Utes drove the Navajos far south of the Gila River. The captured maiden, despairing at last of rescue, tried to scale the rocks of her prison using the vines that grow beside the Pau-to-creeda spring, but she missed her hold and fell a thousand feet to her death, her body striking deep within the green mound, buried there by the force of her fall.

HAUNTED SPRING

"So it is the maiden's spirit that haunts this spring," I said when Martinez concluded the tale. He nodded glumly, staring into the flickering flames. I had meant my words to sound light and mocking, but they rang hollow in the silence of the gulch.

"It is said," Martinez continued after a moment, "that anyone drinking from the haunted spring will be plagued by bad luck. I have experienced this myself, for I once drank from the Pau-to-creeda spring, as you did, and afterward I fell from a precipice and would have died had my body not struck the limbs of a pine tree. Even then it took all the power of a local medicine man who has some influence with the spirit of the spring to bring me back from the edge of death."

"Hogwash," I muttered derisively, holding back a shudder. Was it me, or did the night seem suddenly darker, the shadows more menacing? The murmur from the spring no longer sounded friendly to my ears. "I don't believe in that nonsense!" I exclaimed.

Martinez shook his head, then grabbed his blankets and hurried away from the fire and the haunted spring. He disappeared into the darkness, heading away from the cursed spot as fast as his feet would take him. I had no idea where he'd decided to bed down for the night, and I didn't care. I was staying by the spring. It was just an old Indian legend, I told myself sleepily. You couldn't be hurt by a legend. I rolled myself up into a blanket and lay down to sleep.

I was restless at first. The burbling of the spring kept me awake, and I was uneasily aware that the mound on which I lay was the burial place of the beautiful young maiden who had been trapped here so cruelly. The shadows around me were very dark, and I could barely feel any heat from the coals of the fire at my feet. I shivered. Aside from the spring, there was absolute silence in the gulch. I was used to the sounds of the forest: night creatures, the occasional owl, buzzing insects, the chirp of crickets. There was nothing here but the swirling of the spring and a very soft breeze hissing through the steep rocks above me.

I fell asleep at last and dreamed I was in a sinking rowboat with water pouring in from a hole in the bottom. The leaks sprang from all sides of the rickety craft, soaking me to the skin as the boat began to go under. I gave a shriek of alarm, because I couldn't swim. And then I woke, and realized I was soaking wet and getting wetter by the minute. Water was streaming around me, and the fire had been put out by a gusher pouring forth from the spring. Every fissure in the rock around the spring seemed to have sprung a leak. As I leapt up with a shriek, an inhuman wailing rose from beneath the overhanging rock. The sound raked over my skin like claws, biting deep into my ears like needles. It felt as if the pain would tear the top off my skull. I clamped my hands to my ears as tightly as I could, and I doubled over, trying to cover my aching head with the rest of my body while the gushers from the spring pummeled me with freezing cold water.

Inside my gut I felt fear growing. It was a terrible, lonely fear . . . and it was not mine! The mind touching my mind had a distinct female flavor. I felt her despair, and a terrible loneliness. After a moment, the fear was replaced by a grim determination, and I caught a clear thought from the woman's mind: "Anything would be better than this place. And escape was possible, if she was very brave. If . . ."

Suddenly, a brilliant light appeared above me, and the terrible wailing grew louder, if that was possible. Then it transformed from an unearthly howl to something much worse to my mind. It became the all-to-human scream of a woman. It was a cry of absolute terror, and my head whipped up, following the sound. Above me, I saw a glowing white figure plummeting down the steep cliff. It was a beautiful woman, her face distorted with fear as she fell. I gave a shout of dismay and leapt forward, determined to catch her. Time seemed to slow down. In those terrible seconds it became the most important thing in the universe for me to rescue the maiden, to save her from death. I ran and ran toward her—it felt like forever. She struck the ground less than a foot away from my outthrust arms and disappeared inside the green mound next to the overflowing spring. I gave a shout of despair and fell to my knees on the place where her body had disappeared.

Immediately the light faded, the water ceased to flow, and the terrible wailing died away. I was frozen in shock, drenched to the skin, and shaking all over. Again and again in my mind I saw the body of the lovely woman plunging to the earth just a foot away from my rescuing arms. It was too much for me. I leapt to my feet and ran as fast as I could, trying to get away from this haunted place. It was a dark and dangerous gulch, and my flight ended abruptly when I plunged over a ledge and fell I don't know how far. I felt the bone of my leg snap when I landed, and I lay there in pain until dawn, when Martinez found me and bound up my leg. Nothing about my story surprised him, and he helped me out of the gulch as soon as I was restored enough to limp away.

They've mined all the gold out of that gulch now, but I wasn't the one to do it. I couldn't go back, not even if they'd offered me all the gold in the world. Whenever anyone mentioned the new mine, the face of the beautiful woman flashed before my eyes, and I felt again the terrible fear she experienced as she plunged to her death. And it was a very long time before I took another drink from an open spring.

16

La Muñeca

It is true, my son, that we are descended from royalty on the side of my mother. My many times great-grandmother, she was an Arapaho princess. Yes. A princess. The daughter of a great chief. She had eyes as dark as midnight, a smile bright as a summer day, and long black hair that she wore in braids. Lovely, she was. The richest treasure of her people, so they claimed. And so too thought the young Spanish officer who loved her.

His people had come to this land looking for gold in the late 1700s. And gold they found in the heart of the foothills that lay in the shadow of these mountains. The Spanish expedition hired the local tribe to help them excavate the gold, and it was thus that the expedition leader met the Arapaho princess. He was a tall, intense man with a handsome face and a good heart. He loved the girl the moment he laid eyes on her, and her heart was moved by his kindness toward her people. Modest as she was, it took several meetings before she realized that his kindness toward her had a deeper meaning, and she toppled into love with her gallant soldier.

The couple received the blessing of the chief and were married within a moon of their first meeting. A year later a little daughter was born to them. By this time the expedition had taken a huge amount of gold from their mine. The leader knew it was time to report back to his superior officers in Santa Fe, so they packed up as much gold as they could safely carry and buried the rest in a secret space beside a rock he dubbed La Muñeca—the doll—since it had the semblance of a giant toy. To mark the spot, he took the head of a shovel and wedged it into a crack in a boulder that stood over the burial site.

That night the Arapaho princess was awakened by a bad dream and clung trembling to her husband for a long time. When he questioned her about the dream, she said she had seen angry spirits swirling around La Muñeca, just above the place where he and his men had buried the gold, and the hillside had been filled with the dreadful hiss and rattle of snakes. The princess feared her dream was an ill omen, and she begged her husband to be careful on the trip to Santa Fe. Because she was so upset, he gave his promise at once and spent nearly an hour comforting his beautiful Arapaho princess. It was not so easy to calm himself.

The next morning the expedition leader kissed his family farewell, promising a swift return, and left with his men to report to Santa Fe. The Spaniards made excellent time through the mountains, though the way seemed long to their leader, who was missing his family. They reached Santa Fe within a few weeks, and their superiors greeted their gold with joy and triumph. But when the expedition leader proposed returning immediately to La Muñeca to retrieve the rest of the gold, he was told that he and his men were to report to the presidio of San Miguel de Orcasitas, where they were scheduled to join a two-year expedition up the Colorado River. The young officer immediately resigned his commission, for he would not abandon his wife and daughter. And so he alone rode back toward the Spanish Peaks and his Arapaho princess.

The journey was much quicker with only one rider. Within a week, the Spaniard spied the Arapaho village where he had left his family. His heart quickening with joy, he rode into camp, expecting a lovely figure with a baby in her arms to run out and greet him. But the camp was strangely silent, and the people who came to their doors to greet him could not meet his eyes. He stopped at the door of his lodge and came face-to-face with his father-in-law, the great Arapaho chief. When he saw the expression on his father-in-law's face, he knew that his wife was dead. She had gone to gather firewood in the vicinity of La Muñeca—something she did quite often to check that her beloved husband's treasure had not been disturbed—and she was bitten by a timber rattler. Nothing the tribal medicine man had done could save her from the poison that swiftly overwhelmed her body.

The Spaniard moaned in agony at the end of the chief's speech and seized his knife, determined to follow his wife into death. But a tiny cry from the three-month-old child in his mother-in-law's arms stayed his hand. It was the voice of his daughter. The grief-stricken soldier dropped his knife and stumbled forward, and his mother-in-law placed the baby into his arms. He stared down at the child, already a tiny copy of her dead mother, and knew he had to live for her.

Before the baby princess reached her first birthday, it became apparent that there was something gravely wrong on the mountain. On three separate occasions in as many months, two hunters had near misses with rattlesnakes near La Muñeca, and a third died of a bite. The following month rattlers struck down two children who were gathering wood around La Muñeca. A week later a grandmother died from a snakebite when she hurried to retrieve a child who had wandered too close to the site of the buried treasure.

The night after the grandmother was buried, his beloved Arapaho princess visited the Spaniard in a dream. She warned him that the spirits were displeased. The place where the expedition had buried its treasure was sacred, and the spirits in their anger had set rattlesnakes to act as guardians over the sacred mountain, and over the hidden treasure, which the spirits claimed for their own. She warned her husband that anyone who tried to retrieve the treasure was doomed to die as she had and that the tribe should avoid La Muñeca.

The Spaniard shared his dream with his father-in-law, and word of the curse spread throughout the village. La Muñeca was shunned from that time forward, and the site of the village shifted over time, so there was little danger of any of the children wandering there. The young princess grew to womanhood without setting foot on La Muñeca, and when she married, she kept her children away from the cursed mountain.

But her eldest son was not so wise. His heart was greedy, and he lusted after the gold buried on the mountain. While his mother lived, he stayed away from La Muñeca. But after she died, the eldest son hurried up into the peaks, climbing toward the rock formation known as La Muñeca, his heart burning with desire for the buried gold. Carefully he searched among the boulders until he saw a glint of metal deep inside a crack. And at the base of the cracked boulder he spied a small hole.

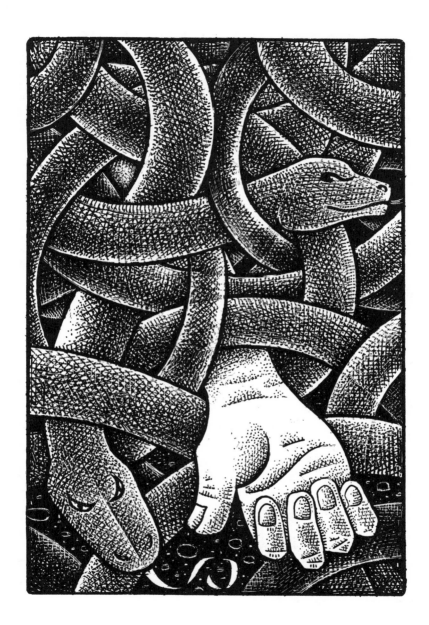

LA MUÑECA

This was the place! He gently teased the rusting shovel out of the crack and used it to enlarge the hole at the base of the rock. When it was wide enough, he reached both hands inside the hole to feel around for the sacks of buried treasure his mother had described. Instead his hands touched writhing scales and his arms were encased at once by slithering, muscular forms. Then his skin was pierced again and again by the fangs of many timber rattlers, whose cool nest he had disturbed with his digging. He screamed in agony, leaping back from the hole, his arms entwined with rattlers. Snakes swarmed out of the hole, rattling their warning as the young tribesman backed hastily away, his body growing feverish as poison from a multitude of bites poured into his system. As he ran, he tripped over a stone and fell to the ground. Immediately his prone form was swarmed by dozens of snakes, which bit him again and again as he screamed and writhed in agony. It wasn't until dawn the next day that his younger brothers found his swollen body in the shadow of La Muñeca.

Even with such a tragedy to act as a warning, there is still one person in every generation of our family who laughs at the story of the curse and searches for the buried treasure. In my generation, I was the foolish one who went to the sacred place in search of gold. And I saw with my own eyes the ghost of the dying tribesman writhing in agony beneath a wriggling pile of timber rattlers. I fled for my life when a timber rattler came slithering toward the place where I stood, knowing that the story of the curse was true.

And so, my little son, I warn you from the bottom of my heart: Do not go near La Muñeca, for it is a cursed place and the gold buried in its shadow belongs to the spirits that dwell there.

17

Roller Skating

I was bursting with excitement. The new roller-skating rink was opening in town today, and I was the manager in charge of the whole kit and kaboodle. It was 1884, and I'd never even heard of such a newfangled notion as a skating rink until folks proposed building one here. Of course I'd seen people strapping roller skates to their boots and whizzing around the streets, but I never thought they'd build a place for them to roll about in. But here it was, a large pavilion devoted to roller-skating.

"It'll never work," my wife said as I carefully adjusted my clothes before the mirror, wanting to look my best on opening day. "Not enough people like to roller-skate. Oh, plenty of people will come to gawk and try it out, but you'll be closed down within two to three years maximum."

"You are probably right," I said, tweaking my collar until I was sure it was straight. "But the money's good, and it beats working in Uncle Alfred's dry goods store."

My wife nodded in sympathy. She knew Uncle Alfred and I didn't get along.

We'd rented rooms right across the street from the new rink, so it was only a matter of stepping outside our front door and walking across the road to get to my new job. I arrived on the scene a few minutes before the crowd, and the rest of the day was a whirl of people renting skates, buying tickets, and buzzing around the new pavilion to the music of a small band we'd procured for the opening.

The whole day was a great big blur, except for a few tidbits here and there that stuck out in my overexcited mind. There were two grand society ladies of uncertain age and vast dignity who had insisted that I accompany them around the pavilion at a stately trot as they adjusted themselves to the newfangled wheels on their feet. And there was a small boy whom I evicted from the pavilion because he kept skating in circles around people, causing them to fall down.

Oh, and there were Treasurer Cook's socks. Those had been a real hit! Treasurer J. Cook Jr. had very large, knobby feet and his demure black boots did not fit into any pair of skates we had on hand. So he took off his boots, revealing a pair of shocking pink and white striped socks, which he then thrust into the roller skates. The striped socks showed clearly through the strap-on skates, and they attracted everyone's eye. People stopped and stared, and some folks bumped into each other and crashed to the floor as they watched J. Cook Jr. skating around the pavilion. He was almost as distracting as the little boy, but I did not dare evict such an important personage, and he soon tired of the new sport and returned to work.

I was bright eyed and far too tired when I returned home from my first day on the job. The pavilion closed late, and my wife was getting ready for bed when I came into our kitchen. She kissed me, pulled a warm plate of supper out of the oven for me, and retired. I ate slowly, trying to calm myself enough to sleep, but scenes from the busy day kept running through my head. Finally I did the dishes so my wife wouldn't complain in the morning, and I lay down beside her. It was no good. I tossed and turned so much that I woke my wife twice. Apologizing to her with a kiss, I rose, pulled on some clothes, and went outside to take a midnight stroll, hoping this would tire me enough to put me to sleep.

It was a fine night with a full moon, and I felt myself relax as I strolled to the end of the street and back. My steps slowed as I proudly surveyed the brand-new skating rink, looming tall against the night sky. I had done well my first day, I thought. And then I stopped suddenly, listening closely, for I thought I heard the sound of roller skates whizzing around inside the pavilion. My eyes narrowed. That was not good. Had some kids broken into the new rink? I pulled out my keys and unlocked the door, ready to summon a policeman if I could not evict the trespassers peacefully.

A lurid greenish-white light spilled over my feet as the door swung inward. I marched inside and saw that the pavilion was lit from corner to corner with no shadows anywhere. It was disconcerting. I had never before seen such a bright light inside a building. And there was music playing, too. I recognized the tune at once, for our customers had been skating to it earlier that afternoon.

I blinked in astonishment as I wiped tears of pain from the glaring light out of my eyes. Where was the music coming from? Had the band returned as a jest? I heard the rumble of roller skates right in front of me, but I saw no one in the pavilion. It was really bizarre. Then, as my aching eyes adjusted to the too-bright light, I beheld two pairs of roller skates whizzing around

ROLLER SKATING

and around the large pavilion. My mouth dropped open in astonishment. The skates were gliding along all by themselves. Two pairs of feet—one large chunky pair and one small dainty pair in kid boots—were expertly navigating their way around the rink in Plimpton roller skates. And—I realized suddenly—I recognized the male pair of feet. They were encased in shocking pink and white striped socks, and the knobbly toes could only belong to J. Cook Jr., the treasurer. But where was the rest of him? How could there be two pairs of feet with no bodies skating around my rink? And where was the blasted music coming from?

I have no idea how long I stood and stared at the whizzing, rumbling pair of skates gliding along to the phantom music. Suddenly the skates vanished in the middle of a twirl, and the ghastly light went out, leaving me in pitch-darkness. I gave a yell and backed out of the rink as fast as I could go. But I couldn't leave it there. J. Cook Jr. lived over on Broadway, and I had to find out why I had seen his feet in my rink in the middle of the night. Heart thudding, I wondered suddenly if this meant he was dead. I rushed to his residence and pounded on the door until the great man himself appeared in hastily donned robe and slippers.

"Thank God you're all right," I exclaimed, still flushed with panic. Cook blinked at me in surprise and pulled me inside the house. I stumbled to a seat and gabbled out my story, waving my hands frantically in the air as I described the strange light and the feet whirling around the rink in pink and white socks. Cook's head jerked as I spoke, and he suddenly kicked off his slippers, revealing the pink and white socks still on his feet.

"I just awoke from the strangest dream," he told me. "I was skating around the new rink with my lovely fiancée on my arm. She was wearing dainty roller skates over her kid boots, and I had on the pink and white socks she knitted. When I woke up, my feet were outside the blankets and were as cold as ice. So I sat up and put on my socks to warm up my feet. A moment later I heard you knocking on my front door."

I stared at the treasurer in shock. "Do you mean I saw your dream? If so, then why did I only see your feet? Why not all of you?"

"I don't know," Cook replied, shaking his head. "This has never happened to me before."

"You mean it has never been observed before," I said thoughtfully. "Your dreams may have manifested in other places we don't know about."

Cook looked gob-smacked by the idea. "Really? You think this may have happened before?"

"It's possible," I said. "After all, a few years ago, who would have believed that spirits could manifest at a séance? But the Fox sisters have proved it's more than possible."

Cook looked thoughtful. "Perhaps we should ask a spiritualist about this strange phenomenon?"

"We probably should," I said, standing up and stretching. "But for the rest of tonight, I'll thank you not to dream about my roller rink!"

Cook laughed and showed me to the door. "I'll dream about chicken pie," he promised me as I hurried out into the night.

I laughed too and then headed home, shaking my head over the strange events. Had I really seen his dream? How else could you explain it? And why the dickens had I only seen his feet? I hoped the spiritualist could explain it when we visited her on the morrow. I sure couldn't!

I shivered suddenly as a shadow crossed the moon and raced toward my front door. "There are more things in heaven and earth, Horatio, than are dreamt of in your philosophy," I muttered aloud, quoting Shakespeare. Maybe tomorrow would bring some answers. Maybe.

18

Tom Barren's Cache

OURAY COUNTY

Things were pretty lively in the saloon that afternoon. Fellers were whooping it up, singing and stomping and hollering. Someone pulled out a fiddle, and a couple of blokes started step dancing out in the middle of the floor. It was fun! I swung my mug of ale in time to the beat and laughed at the antics of the dancers.

After a particularly active song with a lot of stamping and high kicks, one of the dancers fell onto the bar stool next to me and grinned as the bartender dropped a whiskey in front of him. "I hear you're a friend of Tom Barren," he said, downing his drink in one long gulp.

I took a sip of my ale and sized up the feller. He was a blue-eyed dark-haired Irish chap of the type ladies fawned over. But he had a lot of muscle, too, which told me he was no stranger to work. "Tom died a while back," I said cautiously, "around the time them miners were arrested for stealing ore from the Guston and the Yankee Girl. He's buried up in Champion Gulch."

At the time, I had found it hard to condemn the miners who'd been high grading—that's what we called stealing the best ore from the mine shafts where they were working. Those men were slaving away for a measly three dollars a day, just like the rest of us, while the mine owners lived like kings. It hardly seemed fair.

"They say Tom's buried in the gulch," the man said slyly. "But that's not what I heard."

I stiffened a bit and glanced at the bartender, who'd wandered over to refill the feller's glass. "Don't believe you two know each other yet," the bartender said easily. "Mickey, meet Martin Ryan," he nodded to the blue-eyed man. "Martin just moved to Guston from the Yankee Girl Mine." He refilled both our glasses and wandered away. I'd heard of Martin Ryan. He was a hard worker and a fellow Irishman. I relaxed a bit. Martin met my eyes with a twinkle and a wink as he tossed off the second whiskey.

"So what did you hear?" I asked, taking a long draught of my ale.

"I hear it ain't Tom buried up there. It's ore," said Martin. "The sheriff only found six hundred dollars' worth of gold and silver that those blokes stole from the mines. I heard they shifted a lot more than that before they were caught and that they cached it in Champion Gulch and raised a marker to Tom Barren to cover it."

"Interesting, if true," I said cautiously. I considered Martin's words carefully. A cache of ore buried somewhere in the mountains, well that was a treasure trove, wasn't it? Legally belonging to whoever found it? No way to prove it came from one of the local mines, anyway. Martin met my eyes, and I saw the same thought had occurred to him.

"A few of us are going up for a look. Seeing you're a friend of the deceased, I thought you'd like to join us," he said quietly. After giving it some thought, I nodded my head.

We left the saloon as soon as we finished our drinks and were joined on the way by a couple of miners I knew from the Guston. We nodded to one another, but didn't say much as we collected our digging equipment and headed into the late-afternoon sunlight to climb up to the gulch where Tom Barren was buried.

It was a long journey, and when we reached the gulch, none of us could rightly remember where Tom should be. So we scoured the place from end to end. It was Ryan who spotted the weatherboard that said, TOM BARRENS, DIED 1891. He fell on the marker with a whoop of triumph, and all four of us started hurling rocks hither and thither as we dug for the cache. Suddenly we saw a flash and heard a loud crack. Ryan went flying backward, tumbling head over heels. Then an invisible someone smacked me in the head, boxing my ears so hard I saw stars.

"Lord almighty!" I shouted when I regained my breath. "It's old Tom's ghost! Put them rocks back, quick!"

The sense of an angry presence was so clear that the air crackled around us like heat lightning. We put the rocks back onto the grave and raced away as if the devil himself were hot on our trail. The air sizzled as we ran, leaving sparks in my beard and my hair standing on end. I've never made the trip down the mountain quite so fast. Martin and the others were right on my heels, and we all fell into the saloon when we got to town.

The four of us downed drinks as fast as the bartender could pour them. After a half hour, the liquid courage fortified us enough to tell our tale to the bartender. To my indignation, he laughed at us.

"That weren't no ghost. That was lightning," he said. "Storm clouds have been hovering over the mountaintop all day. Yer a bunch of sissies!"

Sissies! Them's fighting words! I'd have blacked his eye right then and there, but Martin pulled me out of the saloon afore I could take a swing.

"Maybe he's right about the lightning," Martin said to me when I'd calmed down a might.

"Lightning, schmightning!" I shouted, enraged. "I'll show him a sissy!"

"Calm down, Mickey," Martin said soothingly. "Forget about the bartender. Let's think about the gold. I suggest we return to the gulch tomorrow and try again."

"I'll try again right now!" I roared drunkenly, storming along the veranda. I fell headlong down the porch steps and lay with my nose in the dust of the road. "What happened to the sun?" I asked the boots that appeared next to my nose.

"It's nighttime, Mickey. We can't go back to the gulch tonight. We'd kill ourselves on the mountain. Sleep it off, and we'll go after the cache tomorrow," Martin said.

"S'right. Go after the cache. Not a sissy," I muttered, allowing him to haul me to my feet and drag me back to the boardinghouse.

The next day passed quickly away. As soon as I finished my shift in the mine, I went to find Martin. We collected our fellow gold hunters and made our way up into the mountains.

We found our way into the gulch and up onto the shelf where Tom Barren's cache was buried. This time Martin made me pick up the weathered headboard. He wasn't taking any chances on another stray bolt of lightning knocking him head over heels. I grabbed the board in both hands and pulled. It wouldn't budge. I hauled again at the marker, and it buzzed in my hands. A bolt of pain sizzled through me. The lightning was back, I thought. Only it wasn't lightning. My dazzled eyes slowly registered a glowing pair of miner's boots standing on top of the weathered grave marker. I looked up and saw rough miner britches, a tattered shirt and coat, and a pair of blazing eyes. It was Tom Barren's ghost. He glared down at me from under his glowing scruff of beard, and I knew he was rat-spitting mad.

"Tommy, lad," I gabbled, dropping the board and backing away. "Good to see you. You're looking very . . . transparent these days!"

"You no good hornswaggling rat-eating blighter!" Tom Barren roared. Two large stones floated up from the top of his grave and hurled themselves at my head. I ducked behind Martin, who took one in the chest and another in the knee.

"Thieves! Imbeciles!" Tom shouted, throwing sand into our eyes and then hurling a mess of pebbles that stung our skin like flies. "May the curse of Mary Malone and her nine blind illegitimate children chase you so far over the hills of damnation that the Lord himself can't find you with a telescope."

A second volley of rocks followed the first.

"Run!" shouted Martin. His voice sounded choked from all the grit he had swallowed. I didn't need urging. That sparking, crackling, roaring maniac dancing in rage on his grave was too much for my nerves. Call me a sissy, but I couldn't take any more. I ran, followed by a flurry of rocks that pummeled my shoulders, back, and arms. I tripped once over a tree limb, did a midair somersault, and kept running. From the sound of

TOM BARREN'S CACHE

pounding feet around me, I gathered my fellow treasure seekers were keeping pace with me.

"May the seven terriers of hell sit on the spool of your breast and bark in at your soul case," Tom roared faintly from somewhere behind me. Oh boy, was he mad!

We didn't stop running until we reached town. I wanted to grab that smirking bartender and run him out of town in tar and feathers, but the other men talked me out of it. They didn't want our fellow miners laughing at the way we'd been routed out twice by Tom Barren's ghost. I could see their point.

"Still," Martin said as we nursed our drinks at a corner table, "old Tom had to be riled up for a reason. He's probably got quite a cache buried under them rocks with him."

"You want to go back and find out?" I gibed from my seat across the table.

"Not me. I value my neck too much," said Martin.

We all agreed.

19

The Piano Man

RICO

He was a handsome fellow with brooding eyes and a smile that set her heart pounding against her ribs whenever he flashed it her way. She wanted him from the moment she first heard him playing piano in the saloon at the hotel where they both worked. It did not matter to her that he had a beloved wife living quietly with him in a small house in River Street and a daughter back East. Whenever she could, she broke away from her duties as a serving maid and lingered in the doorway, listening to him play the piano.

She knew—of course she knew—that she was a comely girl. And she caught the piano man's eye before long. Her flirtatious glances and her obvious attraction to him raised an answering spark. She would pout prettily and insist he play her favorite song. He would cock his head quizzically at her and play a few bars of *his* favorite song just to see her put her hands on her hips and shake her finger at him. Then he would play her song. He resisted her blandishments longer than she thought he would, but soon they were meeting clandestinely in the back hallway of the saloon.

She desperately loved her piano man, but she knew right from the start that his heart belonged to his wife. The thought made her so jealous that she nearly burst with it. There must be some way she could woo him away from his spouse. But how? She tried every enticement, every flirtation, every wile in her admittedly large repertoire of wiles, to no avail. Indeed, he seemed stricken with guilt by their clandestine meetings, and his air grew more feverish, his eyes too bright. He was a known hypochondriac and sometimes suffered from paranoia. He rather frightened her when his paranoia was at its peak, and as time went on, her presence seemed to spark it, as if his guilty conscious was acting as a trigger that brought on his problem.

There came a day when he failed to present himself for his duties at the saloon piano. She waited in vain for him to arrive and finally questioned the other staff about his absence. To her horror she learned that her handsome piano man had taken his own life the night before, leaving two notes for his devastated wife, which said, "Forgive me" and "Better this than be untrue to you."

She was overcome with her loss and fled from her duties that night to weep for hours in her room. She received no sympathy from the staff, for they laid the blame for the suicide at her door. Still, she crept out whenever she could to lay flowers on his grave, mourning him as deeply as his wife.

It was not long after he was buried that she was awakened in the middle of the night by the sound of the piano playing her favorite song. She leapt up when she heard the tune, wrapping a robe around herself and racing downstairs from the servant's quarters with pounding heart, sure it was him. It had to be him! A mistake had been made, and he was not dead after all. But the saloon was silent when she tripped inside and the keys of the piano were still under the lid. She went reluctantly back to bed and cried herself to sleep, missing him all over again.

She was serving in the dining room the next day when she heard her favorite tune again. She almost dropped the platter of food she carried, such was her hurry to put the plates down and run to the saloon. But the piano was still and silent when she got there. Puzzled, she turned away and hurried back to apologize to the fuming patrons at her table.

Off and on all day she heard the tune from the saloon, and it began to haunt her dreams at night. She no longer raced to the saloon when she heard the sound of the piano, but in between her duties she would peek inside and glare at the piano, daring it to play by itself. Once, she thought she saw a gray figure silhouetted against the wood, and her heart thundered inside her chest. Was it him? She blinked and looked again, but the piano bench was empty, the keys were still.

She was bleary-eyed all the time now, her sleep constantly interrupted by the sound of piano music. She was growing to hate the tune that she had once begged for so prettily.

She staggered into the dining room after another sleepless night, her vision so blurred she could hardly see the patrons she was serving. Sleepiness made her clumsy, and she almost fell into a man's lap when she leaned over to pour him some coffee. She righted herself with an apology, but the man's wife glared at her, thinking she was being flirtatious. She turned away, feeling guilty even though all she had done was lose her balance. The woman's jealousy reminded her of the piano man's wife, who had lost everything because of her. For the first time she felt a twinge of guilt about her role in the tragedy.

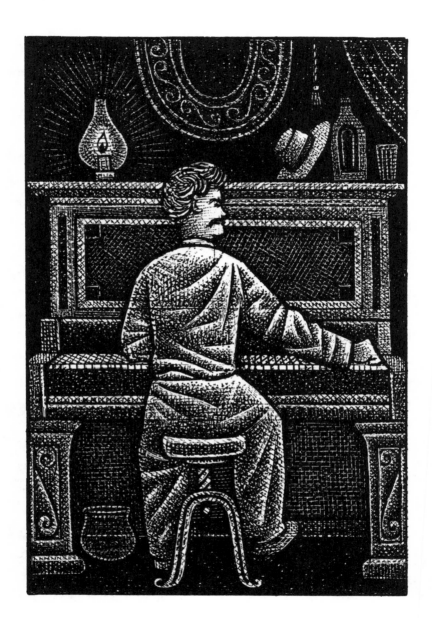

THE PIANO MAN

At that moment, she heard the piano play a couple of bars of her onetime lover's favorite song, followed by a few bars of her favorite song, just the way he used to play it when he was alive. Trembling, she raced across the dining room into the packed saloon, thrusting her way through the crowd, her eyes fixed on the piano. And there he was, sitting on the piano bench. She could see the keys moving beneath his fingers. He was alive. He was alive!

And then the piano man turned on the bench to look at her, and she knew he was not alive. His skin was gray and billowed and writhed beneath the surface like smoke. His black eyes were aflame with hatred, and his hands looked like claws. She stood transfixed. As he floated up from the bench, her skin goosefleshed and her mind reeled under the sheer weight of his rage. She could see the wood of the piano through his translucent body, hear the murmur of the crowd behind her, feel the quivering resonance of the still-vibrating strings of the piano. Every detail burned itself into her mind as she gazed at the wraith of her lover, unable to look away. Then he lunged forward and wrapped his all-too-real hands around her throat, shaking her back and forth in unmitigated rancor. She tried to scream, but the life was being choked out of her, and she could not draw a breath.

The world was turning black when a man suddenly thrust himself between her and the wraith, flinging it back against the piano. Before their eyes the phantom vanished into the wood, and she gasped desperately for air, screaming, "Leave me alone!" at the disappearing phantom.

Almost at once she was surrounded by people who'd mistakenly thought her rescuer was her attacker. She was too stunned to explain; her throat so rasping and sore that she could barely speak. She ran from the room in a panic, and a mirror confirmed that there were bruises on her neck from the piano man's attack. She raced upstairs and packed her bags with shaking hands, afraid to stay another minute in this haunted place.

She heard later that the piano man continued to haunt the local hotels, playing the piano late into the night. Every time the rumor reached her, her throat burned and she again felt his ghostly hands closing over her neck.

She never returned to Rico.

20

The Weeper

DURANGO

The cry woke me from a deep sleep. We'd been white-water rafting all day, and sleep had come easily as soon as I laid down. But I'm a mother of twenty-one years, and the cry of a baby can still pull me out of the soundest sleep.

I rubbed my eyes, wondering whose baby was crying and glanced fondly at my sleeping husband. He lay on his side, snoring gently—something he would deny doing with his last breath. The cry came again, and I frowned as I swung my legs over the side of our king-size hotel bed and went to get a drink of water from the bathroom.

The cry came a third time, as I walked out of the bathroom. I felt a frisson of alarm slice through me. The sound was not coming from the hotel. It was coming from somewhere outside, near the river that flowed past it. Why was a baby down by the river in the middle of the night? Had someone abandoned an infant?

I was putting on my clothes before I finished the thought. I hurried down to the hotel lobby to report what I'd heard to the hotel staff, but the front desk was strangely empty. Should I wait for someone to return, or run to the river myself? The memory of that mournful cry decided for me. If I waited, it might be too late for the child who wept by the river. I hurried out the doors and around the hotel, aiming for the place where I'd heard the cry.

It was a cloudy night, and I cursed myself for not bringing a flashlight. I could hear the swish of the river ahead of me, and I strained my eyes against the darkness, listening. Listening . . .

The cry came again, a soft wordless wail. *It must be the abandoned baby,* I thought. And yet, how was that possible? I was almost to the river, and the sound was clearly coming from the center of the rushing water. How could a baby be out there?

The weeping rose again from the river, and with it came a ball of light illuminating the white tips of the waves rushing rapidly past my feet. The light made the shadows even darker and the water of the river look brown and muddy from the sudden snowmelt in the mountains. I gulped, pressing a hand to my fast-beating heart as the wailing ball of light became the figure of a dark-haired woman in white, floating just above the muddy water. She moved forward in agitation, moaning softly and wringing her hands as she walked. Her dark eyes darted from side to side as if she were searching for something.

Icy shards pierced through my legs, my arms, and my torso, freezing me in place as I stared at the apparition. Please don't let her see me, I prayed fervently. But it was too late. The spirit was upon me in an instant. She stepped right onto the riverbank where I stood and walked right through me. Ice-cold mist seemed to fill me. And then our minds joined, and her memories swept over me . . .

THE WEEPER

It was over in a split second. The weeper was through my body and hurrying up the riverbank before I had time to draw breath. A moment later she vanished.

I crumpled to the ground, feeling the water swishing against my right foot, which had landed in the river but I had been too stunned to notice. Suddenly I was on my feet and running for the car park, fumbling for my car keys, which I had absently thrust into my pocket as I dressed in the darkened hotel room. I had to get away from this place. *Away* was the only thought in my stunned brain.

Ten minutes later? An hour later? I don't know how much time had elapsed before I came back to my senses and realized I was kneeling with my head pressed against the altar in a small church, wailing as mournfully as the weeper I'd seen by the riverside. A priest stood next to me, wringing his hands and beseeching me to speak to him. His tanned face was crinkled with distress, and I realized he had been calling to me for a long time. Slowly, I sat up and wiped my swollen eyes.

"My dear," he said, kneeling beside me and taking my hand. "My poor dear, what is wrong?"

I pressed my free hand to my hot face and gasped: "Do you believe in the supernatural?"

Even in my distressed state, I saw his lips twitch, and I realized what I'd just asked. Of course he believed in the supernatural! He was a priest!

"Most definitely," he assured me. I gave a watery chuckle at his dry tone, and he smiled back at me.

"Will you tell me what is wrong?" he asked, his deep voice filled with compassion. I hesitated a moment. It would sound so strange to say I had seen a ghost. But the burden of memory that the weeper had dropped upon me was too great for me. My mind would snap under the weight of it if I did not speak.

"I saw . . . I saw a ghost," I gasped finally. "Down by the river. I heard something crying. I thought it was an abandoned baby, and I hurried down to the river to rescue it. And I saw this woman walking in the center of the river. She was crying and wringing her hands. She walked toward the bank where I was standing. And then . . ." my voice choked off for a moment. I clutched my tight throat until the words broke free: "And then she walked right through me before I could run away. And oh, Father—she gave me her memories! Her terrible memories . . ."

I broke down again, beating the altar with my free hand. The father grabbed it before I could damage myself. Holding both my hands firmly in his, he said: "Tell me what you saw in her memories." His tone was firm and commanding and seemed to release the pent-up scenes from my mind.

She was in love—desperately in love. He took her without marriage, but she didn't care and he didn't either. He was proud of her and the sons she bore him. He was the don of his people, and he presented his firstborn son to them while she stood beside him, beaming with pride. No matter that a wedding did not take place. As his lover, she lived in the big house and wore beautiful clothes. And her second son was as cherished as her first.

And then the lady came from Spain. The lady was as lovely as the summer breeze, as lofty and noble as the sun, and the lady's family was devout. They would never tolerate the infamous

*behavior in which the don indulged. The don
wanted the lady for his wife, and so he threw
his lover away in a brutal manner that left no
doubt of his indifference. He said that the lady
from Spain was pure and holy while his lover was
wanton, base, and corrupt.*

*She flung herself at his feet and cried out
despairingly that she would repent in front of
the priest and do whatever it took to make herself
acceptable to him. And he shouted out that she
could never be respectable. He pointed to the
two illegitimate boys as the ultimate sign of her
depravity. Then he threw her out of the house, and
his armed men chased her down to the edge of the
river, taunting her mercilessly.*

*She held her two tiny sons by their chubby
hands and kept running when she reached the
water. The armed men turned away, thinking
she would swim across the river and return to
her people. But her mind was in turmoil. The
don's words rang over and over in her agonized
brain: Her sons were the ultimate sign of her
depravity. It was her sons who stood between her
and the don. If they were gone, he would take her
back. She started swimming when she reached the
deeper part of the river, and in the center, she let
go of the boys' hands. She let go . . .*

I gave a terrible wail when I reached this part of the story,
surfacing from the weeper's memories to stare in horror into

the sympathetic eyes of the priest. "She let go!" I screamed desperately. "She let go, and the water swept them away. They were crying and kicking and trying to keep their little heads above the water. They were so frightened, and she *let them go!*" The horror of that moment was so great, I doubled over, pain shooting through my heart, my gut.

"I hate her!" I shouted, pulling my hands free from the priest's grip and pounding both of them on the altar. "I hate her. How could she kill them? They were her babies!"

The priest murmured soothingly to me until I settled down into a miserable ball at the base of the altar. "I hate that I can see her memories," I moaned. "I can feel every emotion that led up to that moment when she let them go, and, Father, in a terrible way it made sense! The don said the boys were the sign of her depravity and that was why he was sending her away. So she got rid of them. Dear God, she got rid of them!" I had no more tears left. I hunched down until my shoulders felt as if they were on top of my heels.

"What happened then?" the priest asked softly, taking my hand again.

"She went back to the don and told him the boys were gone," I said miserably. "He hit her really hard. It knocked her out. When she returned to consciousness, she was lying on the riverbank in the place where she'd drowned her boys, and all her possessions were in a sack beside her. She sat up slowly, taking in all the finery and jewels that the don had given her, and she knew they were worthless. She knew the only things she possessed that had had any worth had just died in the river."

I took a deep breath and continued. "S . . . she started screaming and rocking in horror at what she'd done. And then she went all calm and misty and started walking along the riverbank, calling to the boys, as if they'd gone swimming and she wanted them to come home for dinner. Eventually she tripped over an exposed root and fell into the river herself. She didn't even try to swim. She just let the current take her, and it was a relief to her when she breathed in water and sank into darkness."

I huddle into a tighter ball. Some of the misery had eased with the telling, but I kept seeing the moment when the weeper let go of her sons' hands. It kept replaying over and over in my mind.

The priest gave a deep sigh. "Llorona," he said sadly. "She is called La Llorona. The Wailing Woman. Because she drowned her children, she is condemned to search for them forever along the streams and rivers of the world. And she will never find them, for they are gone."

"How could she do it, Father?" I whispered. "I have two grown sons, and I could never, ever have done what she did." I shuddered as I spoke, remembering the state of her mind in that moment of crisis. *Would I have done the same?* I wondered silently.

"Of course you wouldn't," said the priest reassuringly, and the uncertainty in my mind faded. I knew then that I was stronger than La Llorona. In her place I might have been frightened and sad, but I would never have done what she did.

As I calmed down, I suddenly yearned for the solid, comforting presence of my husband. Grabbing my cell phone, I called the hotel room and woke my him. I told him where I was and what had happened, and he came in a taxi at once and grabbed me in a tight hug when he got to the church. He'd heard stories of La Llorona all his life, and he believed mine as soon as he heard it.

We spoke with the priest for a long time that night, and the sun was rising in the east when we got into our car and drove back to the hotel. My husband went back to bed, but I stood at the window of our room for a long time, gazing down at the river and remembering the way the weeper had wrung her hands. I decided I would call both my sons at college later in the morning, just to reassure myself that they were safe. As I got into bed beside my husband, I felt a pang in my heart for La Llorona, who searched the river in vain for her sons. But she would never find them, for the water had swept them away.

21

The Icehouse

FORT COLLINS

When Percy disappeared late in the spring of 1893, no one suspected a thing. Farmhands in the region were transient. As soon as they heard about a gold strike in the mountains, off they went to seek their fortune. So when Percy failed to appear for his duties on Mr. Brown's farm one bright morning, it elicited no alarm among his fellow workers. Everyone thought he was panning for gold in the Rocky Mountains, and they shrugged off the missing man as yet another victim of gold fever.

Then Ned went missing on the first day of summer. This disappearance alarmed the locals. Ned had a wife and two kids, and none of them knew where he'd gone. He'd left no message, and none of his tools was missing. His wife was frantic, wandering from door to door asking about Ned, interviewing the other hands working for Mr. Brown. But no one knew where her husband had gone. The theory put forth by folks in town was that Ned had grown tired of being henpecked by his shrew of a wife and had been hired on as a cowboy when an outfit passed through earlier in the week. Course, no one in town was brave enough to offer this opinion to Mrs. Ned.

But when old Jeb failed to report for duty a month after Ned disappeared, the men working Mr. Brown's farm grew seriously alarmed. Old Jeb had a crippled wife to whom he was devoted, and he went home every night with some small gift from the creamery or the farm kitchen for her. When old Jeb didn't appear for work, the men sent a stable hand down to his place to see if he or his missus was ailing. The boy came running back a few minutes later to report that the old wife was hysterical because Jeb hadn't come home the previous night. Truly alarmed now, the farm manager sent word of Jeb's disappearance to Mr. Brown while the farmhands started searching the prairie and nearby mountains for old Jeb.

It was the stable boy who found old Jeb. The boy came screaming into the barnyard, shaking so hard he couldn't speak. He just kept pointing toward a coppice of trees a mile distant that housed the family graveyard. The farm manager and several farmhands hurried to the grove, while a dairymaid tended to the poor stable boy, who was violently ill into the water trough.

When the search party reached the edge of the trees, they were overwhelmed by a sickly sweet rotting smell. With his stomach lurching, the farm manager dismounted his horse, which was sidestepping uneasily and showing the whites of its eyes. The other men dismounted behind him, and they moved slowly into the shadowy graveyard. The stench grew worse with each step. Suddenly the farm manager gave a strangled yell and staggered back a few feet, his face ashen. Following his horrified gaze, the men saw a corpse swinging gently from the branches of a huge tree. Its face was pop-eyed and distorted. A vulture was perched on its head, tearing flesh from a ragged hole in its neck. It was old Jeb.

"Get off him!" screamed a farmhand who was a close friend of Jeb. He ran toward the swaying body, flapping frantically at the vulture to scare it away. The vulture eyed him disdainfully before leaving its grisly perch and hopping onto a higher branch. As the farmhand swatted at the bird, his eyes landed on a second desiccated figure dangling from a branch at the back of the tree. This one was fairly seriously rotted, and strips of flesh had been torn ruthlessly from its face, hands, and head. But there was still enough left to identify the figure as Ned.

"Holy Mary, Mother of God," the farmhand cried, crossing himself. The manager hurried to his side and caught sight of Ned, bones peeking through the tattered remains of his skin and maggots writhing between the bones.

"Percy's here too," called the miller from the far side of the tree. His voice sounded choked, as if he were swallowing bile. Percy's body was withered and baked by the heat of a long summer, and the birds had been at him worse than Ned. It looked as if wolves had tried to pull the body down, but they had only succeeded in tearing the flesh from his feet and lower legs.

The farm manager's eyes were bright with rage as he motioned the men back to the horses. "Who would do such a thing?" he asked grimly. The other men shook their heads mutely. Murder. It was murder, plain and probably not so simple.

"I'll go tell Mr. Brown," the manager said finally, with a stern glance back at the gnarled tree standing in the center of the family cemetery. He galloped off in the direction of the huge manse where the owner lived, while the other men stood guard over their grisly find.

Word spread like wildfire through the farms and ranches around town. The sheriff was summoned, and the bodies were taken to the medical examiner for postmortems. The verdict was murder by hanging. Each of the men had been knocked out with a blow to the top of the head. The blow was administered by a hard object the size and shape of the blunt end of an ax. Then the victims were hung from the tree until they choked to death.

There were no clues to suggest why the victims had been murdered. The only thing the three men had in common was that they worked for Mr. Brown. As far as everyone knew, Mr. Brown had no major rivals in Fort Collins and no enemies. Still, it was obvious that someone was murdering Brown's farmhands, and the sheriff and farm manager gathered the staff together and warned them to work in pairs and to go nowhere alone. This made it rather difficult to get things done efficiently on the farm, but fear made the farmhands obey the new rules.

Only one man—the blacksmith, Hardy—refused to go about in a pair. He was a giant of a man who scoffed at the idea that anyone could get the jump on him. He walked all over the huge farm, fearless as a bear. Everyone watched him with worried eyes, and bets were made as to the length of his survival. But it wasn't Hardy who disappeared. It was the stable boy who failed to turn up for work one morning two weeks after the murders were discovered. The farm manager saddled up a horse as soon as the boy was reported missing and led a posse out to the family graveyard. And there was the poor little corpse, dangling from the big tree at the center of the cemetery.

Everyone in town was scandalized by this fourth murder. Many of Brown's farmhands quit their jobs out of hand and fled the vicinity in fear for their lives. Alarmed by this turn of events, the aloof Mr. Brown bestirred himself at last and spoke to a gathering of workers and townsfolk, assuring them that armed guards would patrol the farm continuously until the murderer was caught. This allayed people's fears somewhat, but the farm manager was left to carry on working with minimal staff. It was obvious that something had to be done.

After the meeting with Mr. Brown, Hardy pulled the farm manager aside. "Boss, I've been thinking about the murders," the blacksmith said. "There is something all those men—even the boy—had in common. And you're not going to like it."

The farm manager's face grew pale and grim. "Tell me," he said in a voice as cold as stone.

"You know that little stone building that stands behind the manse?" Hardy said.

The farm manager nodded. "That's where Mr. Brown stores his ice," he said.

"That's where Mr. Brown *says* he stores his ice," the blacksmith corrected him. "But he never lets anyone go near that building, and I've never seen him take any ice out of it. Anyway, boss, I realized today that all four of the murder victims used to walk home along the path that passes the stone building. And I noticed there was a light coming from the window of the icehouse on the night the stable boy was killed." Hardy pointed out the window of the smithy, which overlooked the fields where the stone building stood.

"You think the men saw something going on there, and that's why they were killed?" asked the farm manager.

The blacksmith nodded.

"Do you know who has the key to the stone building?" asked the farm manager.

"There is only one key," said the blacksmith softly. "And Mr. Brown has it."

"Can you make another?" asked the farm manager very softly.

"No, but I can pick the lock," said Hardy.

"I'll go get the sheriff," said the farm manager. He departed swiftly, and Hardy went back to the smithy and made nails while he waited.

It was full dark when the farm manager returned with the sheriff and a posse of townsmen. When they entered the smithy, Hardy gestured toward the window overlooking the field. A quick glance told the farm manager that someone had lit a lamp inside the small building.

"Let's go," said the sheriff grimly.

Faces set like iron, the farm manager, the blacksmith, the sheriff, and several townsmen walked down the path that the four murder victims had taken on their way home each evening. As they drew near the stone building, the men glanced through the window set high in the side facing the path. The interior of the small building was lit by many black candles, and there was a satanic altar set up in a terrible parody of a Mass. The floor of the stone house was awash with the blood of a brutally sacrificed lamb, and Mr. Brown—dressed in black robes—chanted over the slain beast in a strange tongue. He was reading from a heavy book that seemed to writhe with evil symbols.

Hardy gasped aloud when he saw what was going on inside the icehouse. Mr. Brown looked up sharply when he heard Hardy's voice and saw the blacksmith's face looking in the window. With an inarticulate cry of rage, he threw down the evil tome and leapt for the door. In seconds the farmer was on the path, brandishing an ax in his hands. His face was twisted into a grimace of pure evil, and his eyes gleamed red in the faint light of the waxing moon. So focused was he was on the tall figure of the blacksmith, that he failed to notice the presence of the others.

"Hold it, Brown," said the sheriff from behind the enraged farmer.

Brown whirled with diabolical speed and leapt at the sheriff like a tiger. It took three men to bring him down. The farm manager slipped into the stone building, gagging at the smell of blood, and stared at the satanic ceremony. The air seemed to throb with evil intention, making his head ache and his eyes swim. He staggered outside, gasping for breath, and fell to his knees. Around him the townsmen were arguing with the sheriff.

"I say we kill him now!" shouted one man. "You saw that blasphemy in there! What more do you need to see?"

"The law says he gets a fair trial," said the sheriff, but his voice lacked conviction.

"What kind of fair trial did Percy get? Or old Jeb?" shouted another man.

The sound of raised voices attracted the notice of the farmhands heading home to their rest. Within moments a crowd had gathered around the posse and the spiting, raving, bloodstained Mr. Brown. The sheriff was thrust aside as terrified farmhands laid violent hands upon the murderer and dragged him toward the family graveyard. Mr. Brown was still calling demonic curses down on his workers when they strung him up on the tree where he'd murdered four men.

In the days following Mr. Brown's lynching, the air of the farm was heavy and taut with unseen energies, like the moments

THE ICEHOUSE

before a thunderstorm. Workers left in droves, afraid to stay in a place where the Devil had been worshipped so vigorously. When Mr. Brown's heir back East was contacted, he ordered the farm sold and the staff dismissed. The farm was sold, and sold again, but no one ever prospered there, and it was finally abandoned.

There is no trace now of the family graveyard within the overgrown coppice of trees. But folks say you can still see the grisly remains of the murdered men hanging from the tree in the center on nights when the moon is full. And sometimes the red-eyed corpse of Mr. Brown appears among his victims, his body writhing in flames.

When my husband, Arthur, announced that we were going to celebrate our thirtieth anniversary with a trip to the Hotel Colorado in Glenwood Springs, I was so excited that I gave a shriek of joy and catapulted across our kitchen to hug him around the neck.

"Easy, Carol," he said, untangling me before I throttled him. "If you're not careful, you'll choke me to death, and there won't be an anniversary trip!"

"Glenwood Springs," I breathed happily into his ear and then danced a jig across the tile floor. Hot springs! Vapor caves! And the historic hotel where the teddy bear had been invented! Oh boy!

Arthur laughed and looked very smug. He had just scored some major brownie points with his announcement, and he knew it. Of course I wasn't the only one excited by the proposed trip. Arthur was a big fan of Westerns, and his favorite gunslinger of all time was Doc Holliday. Visiting Glenwood Springs would give him the opportunity to spend time in the town where Doc Holliday had spent his final days, taking the sulfur vapors in a vain effort to cure his tuberculosis.

The thought of Doc Holliday made me pause in my dance. Arthur had dragged me to Tombstone, Arizona, a few years ago, and the memory of that trip still gave me chills. I come from a long line of psychics, and the overwhelming sensations I received when visiting the town had interfered with my eating and sleeping. So much anger and death had resonated in Tombstone that it made me physically ill to stay there.

By the time Doc Holliday reached Tombstone, he was a killer many times over and a hardened gambler. His on-again off-again relationship with Big-nosed Kate, a "soiled dove" who set up a brothel in town, was creating so much tumult in his life that he tossed her out of their shared home, only to have her drunkenly tricked by the local Cowboy band into framing Doc as a highwayman.

The psychic impressions I received from the ruthless but charming gunslinger were unmistakable. They gave me a headache each time I sensed Doc Holliday's aura around the town. When Arthur took me to visit the OK Corral where Wyatt Earp, Doc Holliday, and others had staged their infamous gunfight, the smell of gunpowder and the flood of emotions I felt made me faint.

Arthur saw the look on my face and interpreted it correctly. "It will be fine, Carol," he said quickly. "Doc was through with his career by the time he reached Glenwood Springs, and the hotel where he died is long gone. You don't even need to climb up to the cemetery with me unless you want to."

I eyed him for a long moment, and then nodded. "I'll think about it," I temporized. Regaining my good mood, I started making a list of all the things I needed to pack. Arthur beamed, relieved to have passed unscathed over that little hurdle, and hurried off to work.

On the weekend of our anniversary, we flew into Denver and took a railroad trip through the mountains between Denver and Glenwood Springs. Much of the route followed the undeveloped sections of the Colorado River, and the scenery was lovely. We sent our luggage ahead of us on the shuttle and rambled across the river on the pedestrian bridge and past the famous hot springs pools. How I drooled over those pools! The big outdoor pool spanned two city blocks, with lap lanes, a deep end, and a waterslide. According to the literature I'd read, it was kept at a comfortable 90°F to 93°F. Behind the big pool, there was a wonderfully large therapy pool that averaged about 104°F. Steps led down into the therapy pool along the side closest to the brick building, and many people were lounging half-in and half-out of the hot water. I was determined to be one of them as soon as we got checked into our hotel!

We crossed the street at the light and entered the historic Hotel Colorado lobby. What a place! The elegant hotel was filled with captioned photos and memorabilia. The rooms and halls had high ceilings, and the lower staircase was carpeted stone. And it was haunted. I sensed the ghost as soon as I stepped into the lobby. I didn't say anything to Arthur until we reached our suite. Then I told him about the little girl in Victorian dress I'd seen bouncing a red ball on the steps. Arthur eyed me cautiously, trying to gauge my mood. Reading his gaze, I smiled reassuringly. "It's fine," I said. "She's happy and won't bother us." He didn't ask me how I knew, and I didn't feel like explaining that I'd had a brief mental dialogue with the ghost as we walked past her on our way to our suite.

We changed into our bathing suits and headed down to the hot springs to bask in the warm water until dinner. We ate supper in the restaurant on the property and then spent some time talking to the staff at the front desk about the hotel's history, which included visits by the unsinkable Molly Brown of *Titanic* fame and President Teddy Roosevelt, for whom the first teddy bear was created in an effort to cheer him up after an unsuccessful hunting trip. They ended up giving us a private tour, which included everything from the basement to the attic, and told us about several ghosts that haunted the place. When they mentioned the little girl with the red ball, Arthur glanced quickly at me and then away again.We spent the next morning down at the hot springs pool, which made me feel so blissful and relaxed that I actually considered accompanying my husband on his afternoon foray to Doc Holliday's memorial. We decided to walk to the gravesite, so we got directions at the front desk and then strolled out into the warm sunshine. We crossed the pedestrian bridge and headed along Grand Street, following the directions we'd been given. The first block was filled with restaurants, and we took our time, peering in the windows and trying to decide where we should eat dinner.

My mind was still on dinner when we stopped at the corner of Eighth and Grand Streets, so I was completely unprepared for the sudden rushing sound, like the wind before a thunderstorm. The sunny scene before me quivered, and a picture of a grand four-story hotel superimposed itself over the modern structures across the street from us. Then the modern world disappeared entirely, and I was standing on a dusty street staring up at a new building called the Hotel Glenwood. I gaped up at it, my mouth open in shock.

And then the scene shifted, and I was standing in a long hallway, looking through an open doorway at an emaciated man lying in bed. His aura was unmistakable. The man in the bed was Doc Holliday. On the bedside table lay his bowie knife and a six-shooter. Doc's graying hair was tousled and lank, and his mustache sagged along his withered cheeks. His eyes were too bright as they watched a tall individual in a long coat pouring him a glass of whiskey. Doc Holliday took the glass in trembling hands and drank it down with obvious enjoyment. He handed it back, and then gazed down the length of the bed toward his bare feet, which peeked out from under the covers. He gave a wry grimace at the sight of them and mumbled, "This is funny." A gunslinger, after all, was supposed to die with his boots on, not barefoot and lying in bed.

The life faded from his eyes, and I watched him breathe his last. The best gunfighter the West had ever seen was gone, just like that.

Then the whole scene whirled around in a spiral of dizzying colors and flashes and a brief smell of smoke. Suddenly I was back on a busy street corner, and Arthur was anxiously clutching my arm and calling my name. I shook my head to clear it, aware of the curious stares from people passing us on the sidewalk. Arthur sighed in relief when he saw I was myself again. I motioned for him to move on, and we crossed the street together, Arthur still clutching my arm.

"You didn't tell me Doc Holliday died here," I said, keeping my voice casual as I gestured toward the building where the image of the Hotel Glenwood had appeared to me. Arthur stopped abruptly, and the man walking behind us cannoned into him. After mutual apologies all around, Arthur turned to look into

DOC

my eyes. "Carol, what did you see just now?" he asked softly. I told him. Arthur looked dazed, and I took his arm and pulled him along Grand Street, giving him time to recover his wits. After a moment, he glanced sideways at me. It was a sheepish look that I correctly interpreted. He was wondering if he owed me an apology for not mentioning the Hotel Glenwood to me.

"How were you supposed to know?" I asked, answering his unspoken uneasiness. "After all, the hotel burned down long ago."

Arthur jumped a mile and almost knocked into a woman with a stroller. "Easy there," I said, giving the affronted girl a placating smile.

"How did you know the Hotel Glenwood burned down?" Arthur demanded.

How indeed? I decided not to mention the choking smell of smoke and the flames I'd seen whirling about me as I came out of my vision.

"It's a psychic thing," I said airily. It was a phrase I used frequently when I didn't want to explain things. Arthur took his cue from long years of practice and asked no more questions.

"Do you still want to walk up to the graveyard?" he inquired as we turned off Grand Street.

"Sure," I said cheerfully. After my experience on Eighth and Grand, I was prepared for anything, although my instincts suggested that the spirit of Doc Holliday would not be hanging out in the cemetery. And I was right. After a short but sweaty climb, we arrived in a peaceful pioneer graveyard. As I stopped to gaze out over the lovely view of Glenwood Springs, I felt a faint tug on my psychic senses that told me Doc Holliday's body was somewhere in the vicinity, though I was not sure if it was in the cemetery itself or buried at the bottom of the hill. But his spirit was definitely elsewhere.

I left Arthur gazing at Doc Holliday's memorial stone and wandered up to the potter's field, which was full of unmarked graves. One of them might even be Doc Holliday's. As I strolled along, I mused silently about the emaciated man I'd seen in a bed at the Hotel Glenwood. Wyatt Earp once said that Doc Holliday was the most skillful gambler and the nerviest, speediest, deadliest man with a six-gun he ever knew. Doc always bluffed in high-stakes poker games because he figured he didn't have much to lose. Most men didn't want to draw a gun against a dying man. After all, if you shot him, you'd be doing him a favor. And if he shot you . . . well, you'd be dead.

Doc Holliday had a bet on that said worms would take him before bugs did, meaning he'd get shot, knifed, or hung before tuberculosis killed him. He almost lost his life nine times: Four attempts were made to hang him, and he was shot at in a gunfight or from ambush five times. How ironic that he died in bed. The thought sent a pang of sadness through my heart.

Arthur came up beside me and took my hand. "Let's go get some dinner," he said, and gave me the smile that won my heart thirty years ago. I smiled back, and we left the cemetery hand in hand.

Rest in peace, Doc.

23

Graven Image

SILVERTON

Thomas batted irritably at the droplet of water trickling down below his collar. The mine was full of drips and trickles, not to mention the cheerful burble of a stream that tripped merrily along one side of the main shaft. Thomas didn't mind the water, having worked the mines here and in Cornwall for nigh on thirty years, but he hated it when drips got under his collar.

Thomas reached a fork where two shafts met and glanced around for the crevice he'd targeted a few days before. He raised his lantern and saw the small opening above him. Carefully he reached into the pocket of his coat and pulled out the carving. In his callused hand the Tommyknocker grinned underneath its peaked cap, its oversize head too big for the rest of its short body. It was by far the best carving Thomas had ever made to honor the Knockers, who were the ghosts of dead miners returned to watch over their comrades. It had taken him two whole months to get it right, and he smiled with pride as he stretched his small frame to its full length in order to place the carving into the niche in the wall. The Knockers would like this gift, he was sure. They'd been very active in this part of the mine, and such a token as this would keep them friendly for months.

"Nice one," his friend George Kelly called, pausing for a moment from his tracklaying to eye the new carving. "Even better than the one you made last year."

Thomas modestly averted his eyes and shifted his pickax from one shoulder to the other. George straightened and came over to Thomas. "I've got me a bit of pasty here that the Knockers will like," he said. He pulled a napkin-wrapped parcel from his pocket and carefully unfolded the cloth to reveal the thick pasty underneath. He carefully broke off a corner and stretched up to place the bit of meat pasty beside the carving. At that moment, a huge fist came out of nowhere and smashed his hand away from the niche. A second blow sent the napkin-wrapped pasty tumbling across the floor and into the stream.

"Idolater! Sinner," bellowed the owner of the massive fist. "Thou shalt not make unto thee any graven image!"

Simeon, a red-bearded giant of a man who'd just started work at the mine, loomed over George and Thomas, his huge hand raised as if to strike a third blow. Tiny Thomas, who stood four feet, eleven inches in his boots, thrust himself between George and the red-bearded man, his black eyes blazing with fury. George was working a ten- or twelve-hour shift in the mine, like the rest of them, and that pasty was the only food he'd have to eat during the backbreaking hours ahead. Sending his lunch into the stream was a foul trick, and Thomas wouldn't stand for it.

"George is *not* a sinner, and you just ruined his lunch," the small man roared, matching the giant tone for tone. Thomas had a temper that could make a mama grizzly bear think twice before attacking. It rocked the huge Simeon back a few feet. Before he could recover, Thomas shouted: "And that's not a graven image, that's a Tommyknocker. You'd best learn the difference, Simeon, or the Knockers will make your life a misery."

Ashamed of showing fear, Simeon drew himself up to his full, massive height and started forward with a thunderous expression on his face and his pickax in hand. But by now the shaft was crowded with miners, all glaring at the newcomer, daring him to start something. No one liked Simeon much, and he knew it. Simeon's religion was very strict, and he preached repentance morning, noon, and night. But as far as the other miners could see, there didn't seem to be a whole lot of forgiveness extended to those doing the repenting. When even the most innocent of joys was deemed sinful by a religion, they didn't really see much point in it. This callous attitude enraged the newcomer.

The only sounds in the shaft were Simeon's agitated breathing and the endless trickling of water all around them. Then Simeon growled, "Offering gifts to a graven image is a sin. Repent or you are doomed to an eternity in purgatory."

He lunged forward suddenly and drove his pickax into the niche in the wall, destroying in one blow the carving of the Tommyknocker that Thomas had so painstakingly made. Then he retreated down the side shaft at breakneck speed, before the other miners could react.

Thomas stared at the shattered remains of the Tommyknocker in the niche, his mouth working in pain and anger. He was too shocked to move, too shocked to speak. Everyone was shocked. No one disrespected the Tommyknockers. Not in this mine. The Knockers protected them from cave-ins and sometimes showed miners where the rich veins were located.

Sure, they played tricks, hiding a man's tools, throwing pebbles, snuffing out candles. But a gift of food usually settled them down. Simeon's violent destructiveness seemed sacrilege to the stunned witnesses.

Into the appalled silence came the sound of knocking. It started low, then rose high up along the back of the shaft, which lay in darkness. A second knock came from above the stream. Another sounded from the roof. Suddenly the mine was ringing with the sound of knocking coming from the walls, the ceiling, the floors, as if a thousand tiny miners were beating steadily upon drums. It was too deliberate to be random. This was not the knocking that warned of a cave-in. It was the steady, angry beating of the Tommyknockers.

The lights from the candles and lanterns flickered wildly, making the shadows dance over the walls as the knocking grew louder, and louder still. The air sizzled with unseen energy, like the air just before a lightning storm. It made the hair on Thomas's body stand on end. Chills ran up and down his spine as he fumbled desperately in his coat pockets for his own carefully wrapped pasty. Around him the other miners were also searching for something . . . anything to appease the Knockers as the whole shaft shook with reverberations caused by the knocking.

"They'll cause a cave-in," George gasped to Thomas.

Strange, angry whispering came from all corners of the mine shaft, as if hundreds of wasps were swarming. Thomas broke his pasty in half with trembling fingers and thrust it into the niche beside the broken carving. He was almost trampled as other miners hurried forward with their own gifts. One after the other, they dropped bits of apple and pie, and even a few coins, into the niche. With each gift the knocking in the shaft eased slightly, and the whispers abated. Even George Kelly, who had no food to offer, found a penny in his pocket to place in the niche before the ruined Tommyknocker. As George presented his gift, the knocking ceased altogether, and the angry whispering moved down the tunnel in the direction taken by Simeon when he fled.

A relieved sigh went up from the miners when the knocking ceased. Thomas's body was suddenly drenched with sweat as the tension released. The electric buzz faded, and the sense of menace was gone as suddenly as it had come.

Slowly, gruffly, the miners resumed the tasks that had been interrupted by Simeon's attack on George. But Thomas stared down the side shaft where Simeon—and the whispers—had gone.

"George, part of that shaft's been blocked off," he said uneasily. "The boss thought it was unsafe. Simeon shouldn't be down there. Especially not with the Knockers so . . . agitated."

"You're concerned about that fool after what he did?" George asked incredulously.

"A statue can be replaced," Thomas said slowly. "But a man's life . . . well, that's irreplaceable. Simeon may not like the way I practice my religion, but as a God-fearing man, I can't let a fellow walk into danger without doing something about it."

Remembering the sound of the angry whispers, Thomas shuddered involuntarily.

George glared at his friend for a long moment, and then sighed. "I can tell you're gonna go, no matter what I say. So I'll go with you to make sure you don't do anything foolish. If Simeon's in the dangerous section, I'm dragging you out of there, no matter what. No use sacrificing the life of a good man because someone's acted the fool."

Thomas nodded his thanks, and the two men headed down the side shaft, lanterns swinging in the darkness. They were about a third of the way in when the knocking began again. Thomas quickened his step and called: "Simeon! Simeon, come out of there. The boss put this shaft off-limits!"

The knocking grew louder, and George stopped suddenly and made a grab for Thomas's arm. But Thomas, seeing the flicker of Simeon's lantern ahead, was running down the shaft toward it, calling the red-bearded man's name.

Suddenly an invisible presence picked Thomas up off his feet and flung him backward into George. The blow was so unexpected that both men tumbled head over heels, their lanterns flying to the floor. The two miners landed in a pool of water that had accumulated in a small ditch at the side of shaft. Just before the fallen lanterns extinguished, they saw a huge boulder smash down onto the floor, in the place where Thomas had stood just a moment before. Then the lights went out, and the mountain roared around them as the far end of the shaft caved in and Simeon's bobbing light went out.

Thomas and George gasped and coughed as dust from the cave-in filled the passage. A few rocks hurtled past their soggy ditch and bounced away, but the blow from the invisible presence had pushed them out of reach of the collapsing roof. They heard alarmed footsteps racing up the shaft.

"Dear God, that was a close one," George said to Thomas. "It was a good thing you leapt back when you did!" Thomas laughed shakily and replied, "That wasn't me, George. I was pushed to safety by a Tommyknocker!"

GRAVEN IMAGE

George gaped at him and said, "I told you that carving was good. I'm glad you made it!"

"So am I," Thomas muttered as lantern light filled the remains of the shaft. The dazed men were hoisted out of the pool and embraced heartily by their relieved comrade.

"I'll make you another statue," Thomas whispered to the Tommyknockers as he was dragged away by his friends for a look-see by the camp medico while a group of miners started shoring up the collapsed shaft in an attempt to reach the buried Simeon. Remembering the wrath of the Tommyknockers, Thomas was sure that Simeon was dead. May his faith take him straight to Heaven, Thomas thought sadly as he limped out into the light of a spring afternoon that Simeon would never see.

24

Snake Totem

GUNNISON COUNTY

I was five years old when the Snake People stole my baby sister in the night. She was sleeping against our mother's chest when she was taken, and yet none of us heard a sound until morning light spilled into our lodge and we saw that she was gone. The Snake People took three babies and two of the elderly from our village on that raid.

My mother was too hysterical to do anything but weep, so I asked my ashen-faced father how he knew it was the Snake People who had taken the baby. I thought he meant the Shoshone tribe, who were called the Snake Indians by the white men, but he shook his head. "Not the Shoshone, Little Flower," he said wearily. "The Snake People from the mountaintops, those who tend the Snake totems. Come, I will show you."

Father took me to the edge of our village and showed me the place where the brush had been crushed by a heavy body that undulated through the wiry undergrowth in the unmistakable pattern of a snake. The trail was enormous! And it stank with the clinging, musky odor of a huge viper. My mind seized up with fright at the sight of the enormous snake's trail, and I shook from head to toe.

My father gathered me up into his arms, and—proud warrior that he was—wept into my hair. I wrapped my small arms around his neck and wept, too—for mother and for father and for the baby sister whom I sensed, though no one told me, would never grow up. It was not until I was older that I learned that the Snake People used their victims as human sacrifices, lowering them on a platform into the pit where the enormous vipers denned to feed the mighty totems. My stomach heaved when I realized what this meant to my family and me. In my mind I see the gaping mouth of an enormous snake consuming a tiny baby—my little sister. I had nightmares for months after I learned the true story of my sister's fate.

I wanted to learn everything I could about the Snake People, no matter how much it hurt me to hear it. So I went to speak to our medicine man, who told me all he knew about the mysterious mountain tribe. The Snake People lived in the high mountain regions in small groups. Each settlement cared for one enormous snake that was the living totem of their people. The snakes were fed with human sacrifices—usually babies and the elderly—whom the Snake People snatched from tribes straying too near their encampments.

The medicine man went on to describe an attack he had once seen by the Snake People. Several Snake settlements had banded together and descended upon the village where he lived as a young child. He had been out late, fussing over his new horse—a gift from his grandfather—when the horses stirred uneasily. His lovely Paint broke away from his grasp and bolted, leaping the fence and galloping away at speed. He raced after his startled horse, and then stopped when he caught a glimpse of yellow-slitted eyes set a good three feet apart gazing out from an enormous black head. A forked tongue flicked out and in, testing the air. Immediately he dropped to the ground and crawled away from the slithering monster, only to see two more enormous snakes undulating into the pen from the other side. He flattened himself behind a boulder and lay still as death, watching the huge snakes attack the helpless horses, their enormous heads striking out repeatedly in sharp darting motions. Fangs flashed in the moonlight, and the horses dropped dead in a matter of seconds, bodies filled with poison. He could smell the musky scent of the venom from his hiding place, and it made his eyes water.

The terrible slaughter seemed to last forever, but it was over in ten minutes, every last horse slain, save for the fled Paint, which was found three days later in a remote canyon far from the village. The poor animal was so crazed with fear that they let it go. Even the best horse tamer could not have calmed it after its dreadful encounter with Snake totems.

I spent the next five years studying with the medicine man and wise elders from many villages, determined to find a way to protect our own from the Snake People and their totems. I became skilled with herbs and medical remedies, and I learned to speak to the invisible spirits and understand the ways of the animals. Most of all I studied snakes, learning every detail of their lives and habits. By the time I was sixteen, I could calm an agitated rattlesnake and pick it up with my bare hands, and I knew every remedy for a snakebite. My reputation as a wise woman and a healer spread throughout the local tribes, and my services were in high demand.

So busy was I with my studies and my nursing that I had no time to spare for love. Then a deputation from a neighboring tribe visited our village, and I came face-to-face with Black Elk. We were instantly and mutually smitten! We scarcely spoke aloud to each other in the week that followed, but every stuttering encounter was filled with unspoken messages that flashed silently between us. Black Elk finally worked up his courage enough to ask my father for my hand in marriage. My father—naughty man—gave him a hard time before consenting to the match.

We were married in the spring, and in the autumn I learned that I was expecting a child. And that's when a hammer fell on my happiness. The memory of my baby sister and the Snake People closed around my heart, and stress made me ill for many days. Black Elk was beside himself. He did not know what was wrong with me, and I could not tell him.

It was my mother who coped with the situation on the third day. She sent Black Elk hunting and confronted me in our lodge. She scolded me for denying my husband and myself the happiness of this new life I carried. "Life happens, Little Flower, sometimes for good and sometimes for ill. But if we allow fear to kill our happiness, then the Snake People have won." Then she took me in her arms, and we wept anew for my baby sister. Finally I sat back on my heels and wiped my eyes.

"The Snake People will never win," I said firmly, placing a hand protectively over my belly. "We won't let them."

"No we won't," my mother said, equally firm.

A week before the baby was born, a rattlesnake crept into our lodge, drawn by the warmth of our fire. Black Elk almost trod on it. He leapt away with a gasp, as the rattler hissed and rattled its warning. I was huge with child by this time. I sat up clumsily among the elk skins and made soothing noises at the snake, listening to its thoughts. It was upset at awakening so abruptly to a big oaf who tried to step on it (its words, not mine!). I sent soothing pictures of warmth and laziness, apology and the possibility of breakfast in the not-too-distant future.

The rattler calmed down and slithered toward me, suddenly curious to learn who this non-Snake snake was. Black Elk exclaimed in surprise and reached for his knife, but I waved him away and held out my arm. The snake slid up my arm and curled its tail around my wrist. I rose slowly and carried it out of the lodge. The end of its tail brushed my huge belly, and the baby kicked back in a sudden spasm of enthusiasm. I carried my new friend to an outcropping of rocks and settled it down in a warm spot illuminated by the rising sun. It made a weaving motion with its head, and I caught a sudden clear thought from it: "Baby boy." I blinked, startled.

"It's a boy?" I asked aloud, placing a hand on my belly.

"Snake Boy," agreed the rattler. "Snake Boy, son of Serpent Tamer." There was a hint of reptilian laughter in the last two words. Serpent Tamer, I realized suddenly, was the name the rattlesnake had just bestowed upon me. It slithered away under the nearest boulder, leaving me puzzled and a little scared. Serpent Tamer was a name that rang too close to the phrase Snake People for my comfort.

I walked thoughtfully back toward the lodge and almost bumped into Black Elk, who was lurking close by, worried that the snake might bite me. He pounced on me and gave me a huge hug, then escorted me back to our lodge. He'd been coddling me the whole pregnancy, and I couldn't get him to stop.

A week later our son was born. As soon as I looked into the child's eyes, I knew the rattler spoke the truth. Somehow I had passed my ability to communicate with animals on to my infant son, and the first creature he'd communicated with had been the rattler, a week before he was born. We named our son Gray Wolf, and I was the only one who knew my son's secret name, given to him by the rattlesnake a week before he was born.

Gray Wolf was taking his first steps by the time he was ten months old. His favorite toy was a rattle I'd made for him. When he shook it, it sounded like the warning of a rattlesnake. I kept a watchful eye over my little son, waking frequently in the night to check that he was still in the lodge. I could not forget what had happened to my baby sister, though I kept my fear locked away in the back of my mind so it would not disturb the happiness of my daily life.

Gray Wolf was almost a year old when the Snake People descended upon our village on a moonlit night in late spring. We were settling down to sleep in our lodge when a shout went up from the men on watch. "The Snake People are here! Guard your young! Look to the elders!" Black Elk grabbed a knife and spear and leapt outside, shouting for us to stay in the lodge. I could hear war cries and the clash of spears and knives as the brave men of our village fought the shadowy forms of the Snake People. I held Gray Wolf tightly in my arms, a knife ready at my side. I would die before I would let anyone feed my child to a Snake totem. The sound of fighting grew fiercer, and I prayed desperately for the safety of the warriors striving to protect us from the evil that had descended from the heights.

Gray Wolf started struggling in my arms, trying to get down. A moment later, I felt a twinge in my animal sense that told me a Snake totem was approaching. Gray Wolf was making a hissing sound through his lips, and I knew that he wanted to go to the Snake totem. Snake Boy, the rattlesnake had named him, and I could feel his affinity with the approaching monstrosity. Then I realized that the rattlesnake had named me, too. In that moment of revelation, I knew what I had to do. I was Serpent Tamer, and my people needed me.

Holding my struggling child against my chest, I leapt to my feet and ran swiftly through the door, pausing for just a moment to grab the rattle I had made for my son and thrust it through my belt. The Snake totem's presence felt like the heat of the sun on my skin, and I ran toward it. Gray Wolf stopped struggling and made a cooing sound of delight, clutching my braid.

I stomped through the shadowy magic forms of the Snake People, who grappled in the moonlight with the more solid figures of our warriors. My anger must have been palpable, for the opponents hurtled away from me as if blown out of my path by a fierce wind. As I moved toward the outskirts of the village, men came stampeding around the side of the horse pens, shouting in terror. Behind them a nightmare figure towered up and up. The Snake totem was thicker than a boulder and taller than a tree, and its yellow slitted eyes were nearly three feet apart. I caught a glimpse of fangs as it opened its enormous mouth, ready to strike. With a roar of absolute fury, I leapt directly into its path and screamed, "Stop!"

Gray Wolf waved his little arms vigorously and echoed, "Op! Op!"

The Snake totem reared back in surprise, its neck looping into an S curve. Then it closed its mouth with a snap and slowly lowered its head, gazing at my baby and me standing small and defiant in its path. From the village the sound of fighting still filled the night, but there was an uncanny silence by the horse pens as we faced down the mammoth black serpent. It weaved its head back and forth and then spoke directly into my mind. "Little Flower," it hissed in a voice that sounded like a spitting fire.

I drew back in astonishment. How did the Snake totem know my name? It told me how it knew, in a singsong voice that attempted—but failed—to mesmerize me. It had eaten my baby sister, and the totem had harvested her memories, devouring the thoughts from her mind as it ate her flesh. My stomach heaved at the thought, but my anger was stronger still.

"My true name," I shouted, glaring fiercely at the monster before me, "is Serpent Tamer, mother of Snake Boy, and I am not afraid of you!"

I grabbed the rattle from my belt and started shaking it fiercely. It sounded like the quivering tail of a rattlesnake. For a moment it sounded alone in the bubble of silence around the horse pens. And then it was echoed from the ground around me as rattlesnakes slid out of the underbrush, summoned by my call. First there were two, then ten, then twenty. In moments the ground was writhing with them. They slithered around my ankles and feet, and their touch was welcoming and friendly. Gray Wolf babbled excitedly in my arms, delighted by the sudden influx of rattlesnakes. The combined rattling sound thundered in my ears, and the Snake totem lowered its head slowly, eyeing its smaller brethren thoughtfully.

"Leave my village," I said. "Trouble us no more. Make your people find another sacrifice to satisfy your hunger."

In my arms Gray Wolf pointed a pudgy finger at the Snake totem. I felt some kind of exchange pass between them, but I could not catch the words. Then the totem's eyes were upon me once again. "Very well, Serpent Tamer, mother of Snake Boy,"

SNAKE TOTEM

it said. "As long as you and your son inhabit this village, my people will stay away. This is a good place," it hissed, glancing at the rattlesnakes dancing protectively around my feet. "I approve."

It twisted its massive bulk and slithered back into the woods as agilely as any of its smaller brethren. I heard it call silently to its followers, and the shadowy figures of the Snake People poured past us, disappearing into the woods behind their totem. At the same moment, the rattlers slithered away into the underbrush, save for one that tapped its way up my knee. I sank down to the ground and freed an arm so it could slither into my lap. It wrapped its tail around my wrist and looked up at me. "Serpent Tamer. Snake Boy," the rattler thought to us, eyeing Gray Wolf as eagerly as my son eyed it. "All is well?"

"All is well," I said. "Thank you."

The rattler flicked its tongue several times in the moonlight. Then it tapped Gray Wolf lightly on the cheek with its head and slithered off my lap, undulating away under a fallen tree.

Slowly I stood up and made my weary way home, amazed to realize that the entire encounter had lasted only five minutes. We were barely settled into our lodge when Black Elk burst in the door. "One dead, five wounded," he said, embracing us fiercely. "It could have been worse. So far, no one is missing."

"Well done," I said.

I put Gray Wolf down on a blanket and gave him the rattle from my belt to play with. Black Elk fetched my mother to stay with him, so we could both tend to the wounded. Behind us I heard Gray Wolf shake the rattle. The sound made me smile.

25

Desperado

SOUTH PARK

There was blood in the air that spring of 1863. Fear trembled underneath each sentence spoken, sizzled in each campfire built, splashed in every drop of meltwater that flowed from the snowy mountaintops. Someone . . . or some*thing* . . . was killing settlers. A miller on Hardscrabble Creek was shot through the heart and left on the creek bank near his sawmill. The axed corpse of Old Man Harkins was discovered bleeding into Little Fountain Creek. A cowboy was brutally butchered on his ranch near Colorado City. Two men were killed in the Red Hills, followed by the murder of a man in Cottage Grove and the deaths of two men from California Gulch. According to rumor, some of the bodies had been mutilated, shot and then struck with an ax until they were nearly decapitated. Others had their chests ripped open and their hearts cut out. Miners, ranchers, millers, cowboys—there seemed no pattern to the killings.

Terror, rage, and panic filled the residents up and down South Park and the San Luis Valley as the body count continued to mount. Two strangers were slain while traveling the South Park road, their mutilated bodies never identified. A man called Peterson was found butchered and partially decomposed in the waters of Currant Creek. Another chap named Chapin was discovered in a pool of his own blood beside the road just south of Fairplay. Chapin was still breathing when the men found him, but he lapsed into unconsciousness before he could describe his attackers, and he died the next day.

Men barricaded their families behind locked doors, and folks were too terrified to travel the roads by night. No one felt safe. And no one had a clue who was behind the serial murders. Chapin's dying mumbles suggested there might be more than one attacker, but there were still folks who believed the murders were done by some ancient horror sprung whole from the native tales that swirled around these mountains.

Then a freighter came driving his oxen hell-for-leather into Fairplay shouting that he'd been shot in the chest by two bandits wearing Mexican sombreros. Turned out the freighter's wound was nonexistent; the bullet had gotten stuck between Lincoln's Emancipation Proclamation and a memorandum book he kept in his pocket and hadn't pierced the skin. But his story was big news. The sheriff finally had a description of the murderers, and it matched that of a pair of infamous highwaymen known as the Espinosa brothers.

The Espinosa brothers were born in New Mexico under Spanish and Mexican rule, when New Mexicans were given land grants to expand the empire and create buffer zones from hostile Indian tribes. After the conclusion of the Mexican–American War, the Treaty of Guadalupe Hidalgo stipulated that the defeated New Mexicans would keep their property rights. Instead, entrepreneurial Americans implemented a process of chicanery and manipulation of the system that caused the Hispanic people to lose two-thirds of their common lands to the new conquerors. Felipe and his brother Jose were among those who lost land.

Without sufficient land to provide for themselves, Felipe and his brother moved their family to the Conejos in Colorado and settled in the town of San Rafael. But their luck was no better in Colorado. Driven by poverty and desperation, they began stealing horses and robbing freight wagons to feed their starving family. But a fellow Conejos resident identified the masked desperados after one such robbery, and the Army was sent to San Rafael to arrest the brothers. During the shootout that followed, Felipe killed an Army corporal, and the brothers fled into the Sangre de Cristo Mountains.

After their escape the American officials stripped the Espinosa home of all belongings. When the brothers returned, they found their family in distress and without means of basic survival. Infuriated, the brothers declared war and death to all Anglos and set out on a campaign to avenge their family and people by killing as many "Americanos" as they could. And so came the bloodbath that terrorized the entire South Park region, until a lucky freighter reached Fairplay with a description of his attackers.

And now the manhunt was on. A huge posse gathered, led by Captain John McCannon from Fort Garland. The men hunted South Park from end to end for many days, until they found the outlaws' trail along Four Mile Creek. Tension built as they carefully picked their way through a narrow canyon and into a wide meadow some twenty-four miles north of Cañon City. Two horses belonging to the desperados stood at the far end of the meadow. The posse surrounded the meadow and shot Jose Vivian, the younger Espinosa brother, when he came into

DESPERADO

the open to unhobble his horse. The first shot went through his ribs, knocking him to the ground, and a second shot killed his horse. The desperado raised himself on one elbow and fired his pistol at Captain McCannon, who was searching the willow trees for Felipe. Fortunately the desperado's shot went astray. A moment later, the brother of one of his victims shot him through the head, killing him instantly.

By this time, the captain had his sights on the elder Espinosa brother, but he hesitated when someone gave out a warning yell in the mistaken belief that the desperado was a member of the posse. One second was all it took for Felipe Espinosa to throw himself into a ravine and escape.

When they searched the desperados' camp, the posse found the bloodied clothing of more than a dozen men, along with their watches, money, jewelry, and other stolen goods. They also found the knife and ax used to butcher the murder victims.

As the manhunt continued, rumors still flew about South Park and the San Luis Valley. Some folks claimed that Felipe Espinosa was on a religious vendetta, sworn to kill a hundred Anglos for every member of his family killed in the Mexican–American War. Others said that the Espinosa brothers had threatened the life of the Colorado Territory governor, calling for amnesty and five thousand acres in Conejos County to make up for the New Mexican land grant that was stolen from them by the Americanos.

And the body count continued to grow. After his brother's death, Felipe recruited his nephew to help with his vendetta. The Bloody Espinosas kept robbing and killing people all along South Park and the San Luis Valley. A fifteen-hundred-dollar bounty was put on the desperados' heads by the governor and several of the victims' families, but the Espinosas remained at large.

Then a husband and wife were ambushed and murdered on La Veta Pass. A desperate Colonel Sam Tappan, commanding officer at Fort Garland, called in frontiersman and veteran scout Tom Tobin to capture the Espinosa Gang, dead or alive. Fifteen soldiers were assigned to Tobin for the mission, but he abandoned the soldiers within two days, realizing that the Army contingent could be heard coming from miles away.

Recruiting a boy from his own ranch, Tobin set out to track the Espinosas on his own. Finding evidence that the desperados had rustled a couple of oxen to feed themselves, Tobin and his comrade searched the skies until they saw a murder of crows wheeling above the trees where Felipe had butchered an ox. Leaving the boy behind, Tobin circled in and shot Felipe, who fell headfirst into his campfire but came up with his gun blazing. Tobin finished the desperado with a second shot and killed the nephew when he tried to flee.

On Felipe's body Tobin found a journal and letters written in Spanish. When translated into English, the journal claimed the Espinosa Gang had killed thirty-two Americans and intended to kill many more. It was also filled with many pious prayers. Felipe Espinosa appeared to believe that the Virgin Mary herself had blessed his murderous mission.

Tobin and his boy decapitated the desperados and carried the heads in a bag to Fort Garland. Colonel Tappan and his officers were gathered together in a large room when Tobin arrived with his sack. When asked how the manhunt had gone, Tobin upended the sack and let the two bloody heads roll across the floor to the colonel's feet, while everyone else scattered in dismay.

Felipe's head was given to a local doctor, who pickled and displayed it for many years before boiling the skin off and donating it to the study of phrenology. But up on La Veta Pass, the headless desperado still appears at dusk, riding a black horse and accosting all who pass with his Winchester rifle and an outthrust palm.

Resources

Asfar, Dan. *Ghost Stories of Colorado*. Auburn, WA: Lone Pine Publishing International, 2006.

Asfar, Daniel, and Edrick Thay. *Ghost Stories of America*. Edmonton, AB: Ghost House Books, 2001.

Baker, Dennis. *Ghosts of Colorado*. Atglen, PA: Schiffer Publishing Ltd., 2008.

Battle, Kemp P. *Great American Folklore*. New York: Doubleday & Company, Inc., 1986.

Botkin, B. A., ed. *A Treasury of American Folklore*. New York: Crown, 1944.

Brunvand, Jan Harold. *The Choking Doberman and Other Urban Legends*. New York: W. W. Norton, 1984.

———. *The Vanishing Hitchhiker*. New York: W. W. Norton, 1981.

Byrne, Charles. *Colorado Legends: Ghosts of the Cripple Creek Mining District*. LegendsofAmerica.com. Accessed 9/26/2010 at www.legendsofamerica.com/ co-cripplecreekghosts.html.

Clifton, Chas S. *Ghost Tales of Cripple Creek*. Colorado Springs, CO: Little London Press, 1983.

Coffin, Tristram P., and Hennig Cohen, eds. *Folklore in America*. New York: Doubleday& AMP, 1966.

————. *Folklore from the Working Folk of America*. New York: Doubleday, 1973.

Cohen, Daniel, and Susan Cohen. *Hauntings & Horrors*. New York: Dutton Children's Books, 2002.

Crutchfield, James A. *It Happened in Colorado*. Guilford, CT: TwoDot, 2008.

Davidson, Levette J., and Forrester Blake. *Rocky Mountain Tales*. Norman: University of Oklahoma Press, 1947.

Dorson, R. M. *America in Legend*. New York: Pantheon Books, 1973.

Downer, Deborah L. *Classic American Ghost Stories*. Little Rock, AR: August House Publishers, Inc., 1990.

Editors of *Life*. *The Life Treasury of American Folklore*. New York: Time Inc., 1961.

Erdoes, Richard, and Alfonso Ortiz. *American Indian Myths and Legends*. New York: Pantheon Books, 1984.

Espinosa, Aurelio M. *The Folklore of Spain in the American Southwest*. Norman: University of Oklahoma Press, 1985.

Fay, Abbott. *I Never Knew That about Colorado*. Ouray, CO: Western Reflections Inc., 1997.

Flanagan, J. T., and A. P. Hudson. *The American Folk Reader*. New York: A. S. Barnes & Co., 1958.

Friggens, Myriam. *Tales, Trails and Tommyknockers*. Boulder, CO: Johnson Books, 1979.

Garcez, Antonio R. *Colorado Ghost Stories*. Placitas, NM: Red Rabbit Press, 2008.

Getz, Charmaine Ortega. *Weird Colorado*. New York: Sterling Publishing Co., Inc., 2010.

Greenway, John, comp. *Folklore of the Great West*. Palo Alto, CA: American West Publishing Company, 1969.

Grout, Pam. *Colorado Curiosities*. Guilford, CT: Globe Pequot Press, 2006.

Hafnor, John. *Strange But True, Colorado*. Fort Collins, CO: Lone Pine Productions, 2005.

Hansford, Nancy. *Northern Colorado Ghost Stories*. Fort Collins, CO: Indian Hills Book Works, 2005.

Hauck, Dennis William. *Haunted Places: The National Directory*. New York: Penguin Books, 1994.

Hill, Alice Polk. *Tales of the Colorado Pioneers*. Denver, CO: Pierson & Gardener, 1884.

Hoig, Stan. *The Sand Creek Massacre*. Norman: University of Oklahoma Press, 1961.

Kutz, Jack. *Mysteries & Miracles of Colorado*. Corrales, NM: Rhombus Publishing Company, 1993.

Leach, M. *The Rainbow Book of American Folk Tales and Legends*. New York: The World Publishing Co., 1958.

Leeming, David, and Jake Pagey. *Myths, Legends, & Folktales of America*. New York: Oxford University Press, 1999.

Mac Iver, Kathi. *Gambling Ghosts*. Cripple Creek, CO: Columbine Press, 2004.

———. *Ghosts of Bennett Avenue*. Cripple Creek, CO: Columbine Press, 2000.

———. *Ghosts of the Mining District*. Cripple Creek, CO: Columbine Press, 2003.

———. *Haunted Inns*. Cripple Creek, CO: Columbine Press, 1998.

Martin, MaryJoy. *Something in the Wind*. Boulder, CO: Pruett Publishing Company, 2001.

———. *Twilight Dwellers*. Boulder, CO: Pruett Publishing Company, 2003.

Mott, A. S. *Ghost Stories of America, Vol. II*. Edmonton, AB: Ghost House Books, 2003.

Murphy, Jan. *Mysteries and Legends of Colorado*. Guilford, CT: TwoDot, 2007.

Murray, Earl. *Ghosts of the Old West*. New York: Tor Books, 1988.

National Park Service. *Sand Creek Massacre National Historic Site*. NPS.gov. Accessed 9/25/2010 at www.nps.gov/sand/upload/Flyer.pdf.

Norman, Michael, and Beth Scott. *Historic Haunted America*. New York: Tor Books, 1995.

Peck, Catherine, ed. *A Treasury of North American Folk Tales*. New York: W. W. Norton, 1998.

Polley, J., ed. *American Folklore and Legend*. New York: Reader's Digest Association, 1978.

Reevy, Tony. *Ghost Train!* Lynchburg, VA: TLC Publishing, 1998.

Roberts, Nancy. *Ghosts of the Wild West*. Columbia: University of South Carolina Press, 2008.

Rule, Leslie. *Coast to Coast Ghosts*. Kansas City, KS: Andrews McMeel Publishing, 2001.

Schwartz, Alvin. *Scary Stories to Tell in the Dark*. New York: Harper Collins, 1981.

Shirley, Gayle C. *More Than Petticoats: Remarkable Colorado Women*. Guilford, CT: TwoDot, 2002.

Skinner, Charles M. *American Myths and Legends,* Vol. 1. Philadelphia: J. B. Lippincott, 1903.

———. *Myths and Legends of Our Own Land*, Vol. 1 & 2. Philadelphia: J. B. Lippincott, 1896.

Smith, Barbara. *Ghost Stories of the Rocky Mountains*. Auburn, WA: Lone Pine Publishing, 1999.

———. *Ghost Stories of the Rocky Mountains,* Vol. 2. Auburn, WA: Ghost House Books, 2003.

Sneed, F. Dean. *The Phantom Train and Other Ghostly Legends of Colorado*. Lakewood, CO: Dream Weavers Publishing Co., 1992.

Spence, Lewis. *North American Indians: Myths and Legends Series*. London: Bracken Books, 1985.

Students of Haskell Institute. *Myths, Legends, Superstitions of North American Indian Tribes.* Cherokee, NC: Cherokee Publications, 1995.

Torrez, Miguel A. *Espinosa Brothers.* New Mexico Office of the State Historian. Newmexicohistory.org. Accessed 9/26/2010 at www.newmexicohistory.org/filedetails .php?fileID=21275.

Weiser, Kathy. *Old West Legends: The Bloody Espinosas— Terrorizing Colorado.* LegendsofAmerica.com. Accessed 9/26/2010 at www.legendsofamerica.com/outlaw-espinosagang.html.

Westerberg, Ann. *Castles of Colorado.* Boulder, CO: Johnson Books, 2008.

Young, Richard, and Judy Dockrey. *Ghost Stories from the American Southwest.* Little Rock, AR: August House, Inc., 1991.

Zeitlin, Steven J., Amy J. Kotkin, and Holly Cutting Baker. *A Celebration of American Family Folklore.* New York: Pantheon Books, 1982.

About the Author

S. E. Schlosser has been telling stories since she was a child, when games of "let's pretend" quickly built themselves into full-length tales acted out with friends. A graduate of Houghton College, the Institute of Children's Literature, and Rutgers University, she created and maintains the award-winning website Americanfolklore.net, where she shares a wealth of stories from all fifty states, some dating back to the origins of America. Sandy spends much of her time answering questions from visitors to the site. Many of her favorite e-mails come from other folklorists who delight in practicing the old tradition of who can tell the tallest tale.

About the Illustrator

Artist Paul Hoffman trained in painting and printmaking, with his first extensive illustration work on assignment in Egypt, drawing ancient wall reliefs for the University of Chicago. His work graces books of many genres—children's titles, textbooks, short story collections, natural history volumes, and numerous cookbooks. For *Spooky Colorado,* he employed a scratchboard technique and an active imagination.